Practical UI Patterns for Design Systems

Fast-Track Interaction Design for a Seamless User Experience

Diana MacDonald

Apress®

Practical UI Patterns for Design Systems

Diana MacDonald
Victoria, VIC, Australia

ISBN-13 (pbk): 978-1-4842-4937-6   ISBN-13 (electronic): 978-1-4842-4938-3
https://doi.org/10.1007/978-1-4842-4938-3

Managing Director, Apress media LLC: Welmoed Spahr
Acquisitions Editor: Louise Corrigan
Development Editor: James Markham
Coordinating Editor: Nancy Chen

Cover designed by eStudioCalamar

Cover image designed by Freepik (www.freepik.com)

Distributed to the book trade worldwide by Springer Science+Business Media New York, 233 Spring Street, 6th Floor, New York, NY 10013. Phone 1-800-SPRINGER, fax (201) 348-4505, e-mail orders-ny@springer-sbm.com, or visit www.springeronline.com. Apress Media, LLC is a California LLC and the sole member (owner) is Springer Science + Business Media Finance Inc (SSBM Finance Inc). SSBM Finance Inc is a Delaware corporation.

For information on translations, please e-mail rights@apress.com, or visit http://www.apress.com/rights-permissions.

Apress titles may be purchased in bulk for academic, corporate, or promotional use. eBook versions and licenses are also available for most titles. For more information, reference our Print and eBook Bulk Sales web page at http://www.apress.com/bulk-sales.

Any source code or other supplementary material referenced by the author in this book is available to readers on GitHub via the book's product page, located at www.apress.com/978-1-4842-4937-6. For more detailed information, please visit http://www.apress.com/source-code.

Printed on acid-free paper

In loving memory of Phillip MacDonald. Thanks for introducing me to the wild world of wordsmithing.

Table of Contents

About the Author

 **Diana MacDonald** is a Melbourne product designer, raised in the tropical north of Australia. She has relished the tech industry for over a decade, exploring the digital space with progressive organizations like Culture Amp, Bellroy, and SitePoint. At Culture Amp, she led the new design systems team to accelerate UI design and development. She values inclusive and remarkable stories. You can find out more about her on her LinkedIn profile (`www.linkedin.com/in/diana-macdonald-didoesdigital`) and contact her via Twitter (`https://twitter.com/didoesdigital`).

About the Technical Reviewer

Katherine Joyce is a passionate designer and developer with over 7 years of experience having worked across the financial and government sectors. She creates innovative, intuitive customer experiences and is an advocate of accessible design. As Lead UX/UI Designer at Alt Labs, she is leading the UX vision and crafting beautiful solutions driven by user needs. In her previous role she worked as a Senior UX/UI Designer for Accenture, promoting accessible design in government services and helping automate legacy processes to improve the customer journey. She has also spent over 5 years with AXA Insurance as an Application Support Software Developer where she fixed bugs in legacy financial systems, debugged issues with browser compatibility, and suggested improvements to customer-facing journeys. She is passionate about advocating accessible design and mentoring those who would like to have a career in design or development.

Acknowledgments

Thanks to all the fabulous people involved in bringing this book to life, including the friends and associates who encouraged me and gave me feedback. Thanks to Simon Mackie and Darin Dimitroff in helping me start this book. Thanks to Wesley Moore, who was with me through all of it.

Special thanks to the folks at Apress who made this book possible.

Introduction

Right now, design systems are flourishing, evolving. Each product or web site is no longer crafted in isolation, but as part of a larger conversation, in a social web, among chatbots and machine learning. It is our duty to ensure every piece of the system speaks to each other, from the components to the people, fluently and eloquently. Thanks to the shift toward "modular design," we see harmonious experiences composed from the ground up of independent modules, such as videos or articles that stand well on their own and yet can also be arranged to fit cohesively into a larger whole. This is only possible when we use a consistent language for designing modules in a system so that every part delights and the whole resonates.

Peacock feathers consist of fractal patterns, as you can see in Figure 0-1.

Figure 0-1. *Photo of a peacock displaying its train*

Here you can see the beauty of the peacock's feathers emerges from the repeated pattern presented together.

My hope is for this book to serve as a guide to designers and makers toward strong foundations upon which we build. With a solid grounding, we can spend more time remixing our ideas into tailored and personalized experiences. We can spend more time exploring the cutting edge, innovating, and crafting beautiful user experiences.

Who should read this book

This book is for designers, developers, marketers, and makers familiar with the basics of building the Web who want to produce better user experiences in digital products. This book will help you learn how to discern good from bad, build on existing communities of practice, and dig deep into fundamentals.

What you'll find in this book

This book offers a concise guide to UI patterns: the tested, proven general mechanisms for solving recurring user interface problems, so that you don't have to reinvent the wheel and can instead focus on designing solutions to the unique problems in your business.

You'll find a smattering of code samples or visual examples throughout the book—only as much as is needed to demonstrate the idea and get you started. You'll also find

- Methods for discovering, evaluating, and implementing patterns according to best practices

- Specific examples of real-world, business-critical UI patterns, including onboarding new users, information seeking and social sharing, as well as e-commerce purchase journeys

- Vocabulary to help you match solutions to problems

- Overview of the digital landscape and resources for further learning

Chapters 2 and 3 explore user signup and onboarding to highlight the process of discovering, evaluating, and understanding patterns through the theme of finding, reading, and sharing information.

Chapters 4 and 5 will cover how to consistently apply solid patterns through design systems and pattern libraries and how to avoid anti-patterns.

Finally, we'll explore mixing and matching patterns for e-commerce in depth. This is where the magic happens. Most of the book will focus on potential solutions, so you can choose the right tool for your problems. This chapter, however, will explore a specific problem space and apply pattern solutions to these problems.

What you won't find in this book

In the digital space, there's a lot of crossover among software engineering, visual design, and information architecture. While these fields have their own rich heritage and history behind them that can inform digital interactions, we'll be avoiding them because that's far too much to cover in one book. However, I strongly encourage everyone to pursue information elsewhere to learn the history of their field of practice as well as the relevant disciplines that came before. For example, while copywriters and content strategists on the Web face uniquely digital challenges writing blogs, RSS feeds, tweets, and cross-channel content, they can learn immense amounts from journalists, librarians, and traditional marketers as some challenges remain the same as those found in these preexisting fields. I'll touch on some copywriting practices for UI later on, but if you spend most of your day writing, you'll want to dig further into these fields.

This book won't cover exhaustive lists of available patterns for all scenarios. There is no complete code library or complete collection of design assets. I will only mention some particular resources, pattern libraries, and showcases that will help you find further extensive collections of patterns for different contexts. I'll also point out common names for patterns that differ across libraries.

How to use this book

Patterns are neat because they elegantly package up all the things you need to know about interface and interaction design. They help you grow into the field. They are useful resources that you can refer back to (you don't need to memorize all of them from the start). If you have the general gist of patterns available and instant access to all of them, all you need to do is look up the pattern you need when it comes time to solve a problem. If you know a handful of relevant, similar patterns, you can look them all up and weigh them one by one.

Use this book to learn how to recognize traits across seemingly unrelated patterns and how they similarly solve problems (e.g., continuous scrolling, tabs, and pagination might have more in common than you think). Then you can start with a problem space (whether driven by stakeholder engagement, user research, or technology), clarify the problem according to real user needs, validate them, then translate those needs into pattern solutions.

Use this book to learn how to communicate UI design solutions. Most of this book will be more valuable to people new to the practice of web and product design as they develop their vocabulary to discuss interface patterns. It may, however, also help experts learn how to share their solutions as they learn how to mentor.

This book will show you concrete examples of how to discover UI patterns, evaluate patterns, and communicate solutions to design problems and user needs. Use this book as a starting point for your journey into making digital user interfaces.

CHAPTER 1

Introducing UI patterns

To help you create intuitive products, this chapter will introduce UI patterns and highlight why they're important and valuable.

What's a UI pattern?

A **pattern** is a recurring solution to a problem in a context.

I like to think of patterns as models: a pattern has a structure and can be easily used to help you solve a problem faster than building from scratch. They have a consistent and recognizable form, as well as a method of being referenced, such as a memorable name. In knitting, you might choose a pattern from a book to help you make a sweater with good sleeves, noting that some sweaters are more ornamentally complex than others. In origami, you might use a folding pattern to produce a complex sculpture from basic origami folds, such as the *orizuru* (折鶴) or paper crane shown in Figure 1-1.

© Diana MacDonald 2019
D. MacDonald, *Practical UI Patterns for Design Systems*,
https://doi.org/10.1007/978-1-4842-4938-3_1

Figure 1-1. *Photo of paper cranes by Rebecca Freeman*

While you might create an *orizuru* using a proven solution, there are many ways to fold a paper crane with varying levels of ornamentation, like a flapping crane or consecutive cranes.

UI patterns (user interface patterns) are found in the digital sphere of web sites, applications, native mobile apps, and other software or devices. They provide a language for discussing interactive design. They suggest function, interaction, and intent. UI patterns document reusable parts of an interface that share a purpose.

To understand UI patterns (and how they differ from components), let's explore some ideas from the UI framework, Bootstrap. First, we'll look at the thumbnails component (`https://getbootstrap.com/docs/3.4/components/#thumbnails`) from version 3 of the framework, as shown in Figure 1-2, before circling back to what makes a UI pattern.

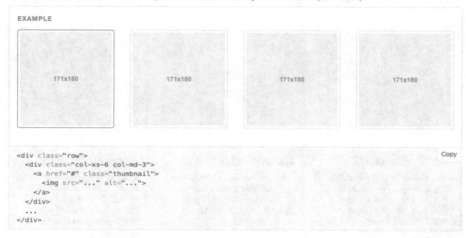

Figure 1-2. *Screenshot of Bootstrap 3's thumbnails component default example*

The **thumbnails** pattern presents small image previews in a collection where each image is linked to a larger resource, such as a high-resolution version of the image. If the thumbnail is a preview of a product, it will link to the product detail page. If it is a thumbnail of a video, it will link to the video player to watch the video. The key features of the thumbnails pattern are as follows:

- Small images.

- Linked resources.

- It represents a collection.

You'll frequently find images in this pattern shown alongside a title or description, as shown in Figure 1-3.

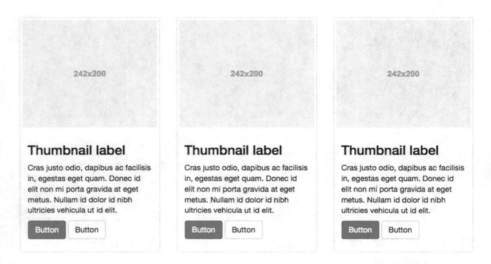

Figure 1-3. *Screenshot of Bootstrap 3's thumbnails component with custom content*

In Bootstrap 4, however, you'll find that this component's been replaced by the *card* component (`https://getbootstrap.com/docs/4.3/components/card/`) using an image, title, text, and link, as shown in Figure 1-4.

Figure 1-4. *Screenshot of Bootstrap 4's card component*

This change more clearly separates the thumbnail's purpose of previewing visual content—a *content pattern*—from the card layout's purpose of segmenting content using repeating containers for images and text—a *display pattern*. The shift toward the display pattern makes sense for a flexible UI framework with built components. We'll learn more about components in Chapter 4.

UI patterns are more abstract than visual style. While patterns can often be identified by visual similarity, these components demonstrate it's not always so easy: a pattern describes behavior, which can be divorced from easily identifiable visual presentation. You can, for example, apply a strong, dramatic visual style or a subtle, muted flavor to a thumbnail collection.

Note   You might also see reference to **user flow patterns** or **strategic patterns** when a UI pattern spans multiple pages, like in the lazy signup pattern in Chapter 2. Similarly, you might read about **behavioral patterns**, **persuasive patterns**, or **social patterns**, where the characteristic behavior presents information, shares a message, or persuades a human, like in the good defaults pattern in Chapter 2.

Elements of a UI pattern

A UI pattern is defined by three ingredients:

- A **named solution** describing *what* the pattern does

- The **problem** the user is facing or *why* this pattern is needed

- The **context** for *when* to use the pattern

For our thumbnail example

- The named solution "thumbnails" suggests a collection of small image previews linked to larger resources.

- The user's problem is navigating a large collection of content and selecting only the items they want.

- The context is when the user needs a preview before deciding—before downloading a large file or committing to watching an entire movie. You'll often find thumbnails on product range pages or search result listings before you've decided which item to drill in on. In contrast, product or detail pages need fewer thumbnails because that product or item is what you came to see so they can be shown in full without a thumbnail.

As you can see in Figure 1-5, Pinterest uses thumbnails in their visual discovery product.

Figure 1-5. *Screenshot of Pinterest thumbnails*

If Pinterest continuously loaded high-resolution images at their full size instead of thumbnails, that would slow down an otherwise immersive experience. Pinterest needs to present thumbnails to facilitate smooth browsing to help people discover ideas.

In a large collection like that, you won't know what image will appear next or if it's something you want to see in detail. By using thumbnails, you can quickly browse a larger set of choices before zooming in on particularly interesting items.

Figure 1-6 shows an Adidas product with thumbnails.

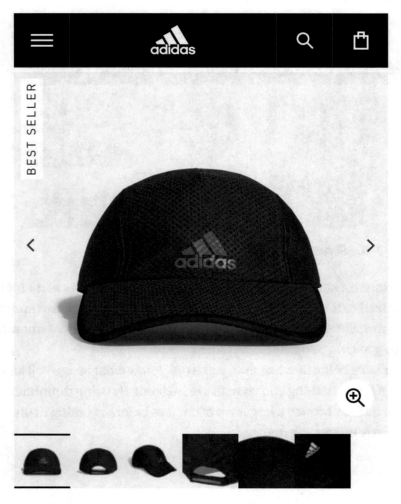

Figure 1-6. *Screenshot of Adidas's product images with thumbnails*

Each small image (thumbnail) in this collection shows a preview of a product photo, linking to a larger photo. Unlike the Pinterest example, here the thumbnails are presented at the same time as the linked item.

The selected thumbnail is indicated by different styling (black borders above and below), while the larger photo is shown.

Warby Parker glasses, on the other hand, need no thumbnails to flick between product images, as shown in Figure 1-7.

Figure 1-7. *Screenshot of Warby Parker's product images with no thumbnails*

These images are the main subject of the page. There are fewer images to browse than most thumbnail collections (just three photos), so smaller previews would not save you much time. You can also predict what the next photo will be: the same glasses from another angle. You might as well jump straight to it than fill up the page with tiny thumbnails. This is an example of when you *don't* need thumbnails.

Other pattern details

When describing a UI pattern, some people also specify these details:

- Why?

    - Explanation of how it solves the problem

    - Supporting principles, such as usability principles

- - User research and other evidence

  - Motivation

- Examples

- How it works

- Consequences

  - Trade-offs and drawbacks

  - Result context and expected improvements

- Implementation details

- Sample code or design assets

- Known uses "in the wild"

- Author or resident expert

- Related patterns

- Alternative names or aliases

- Links to more resources

These tend to be used to elaborate on the three main components—solution, problem, and context. Particularly—and importantly—it is common to suggest alternative, related patterns of interest in the context part of a pattern to clarify when *not* to use the pattern. I note these here so you may recognize them when you see them elsewhere and can consider them for yourself if you find yourself writing a pattern.

A specific collection of patterns for a project is often called a **pattern library**. Pattern libraries give teams a common language to improve their design processes. We'll discuss pattern libraries further in Chapter 4.

Why care about patterns?

UI patterns compare approaches, distilling the considerations and successes of designers before you. Knowing the patterns and understanding the decisions that went into them let you take advantage of the mounting wisdom of whole generations and industries that brought about these patterns, without reinventing the wheel. The small, reusable UI solutions found in these patterns can then be composed together to build cohesive, intuitive experiences that resonate with people.

Let's look at some of the other benefits of learning UI patterns.

Design efficiently

Knowing patterns can help you design efficiently by quickly recognizing the best tool for the job, understanding the value of different solutions, and solving the largest number of problems at once. For example, an autocomplete search box might help your site visitors navigate your site content, recognize the term they're looking for without knowing the exact name or spelling, and select a result after only typing a few characters without needing to waste energy typing in the full search term. By learning about the autocomplete UI pattern, you'll more quickly recognize when you need to use it, and likewise with all UI patterns. For example, if you need to redesign the navigation for a catalog of products by expanding the existing horizontal dropdown menu into a multilevel one, you can see how an autocomplete search box might solve the problem better. We'll look at autocomplete again in Chapter 3.

You can even recognize patterns across evolving technology. Compare the hated "Clippy" (`www.theatlantic.com/technology/archive/2015/06/clippy-the-microsoft-office-assistant-is-the-patriarchys-fault/396653/`) Microsoft Office assistant to Slack's chatbot called Slackbot, shown in Figure 1-8.

11

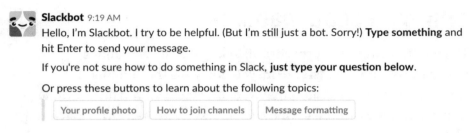

Figure 1-8. *Screenshot of Slackbot introducing itself*

As conversational UIs have developed, we've seen some drastic changes in how we interact with technology; however, we've also noticed some similarities. You can see some familiar patterns, including identity and profile information, private chat, and feed updates. Increasing your familiarity with diverse patterns will help you efficiently solve design problems you face in new user interfaces, especially if you understand the underlying usability principles and can adapt patterns to new contexts.

Consistency and familiarity

Using familiar patterns lets you foster predictability. The familiar idea of **drag and drop** lets you directly manipulate an object by dragging and dropping it. A common use of drag and drop is to upload an image by dragging it from your computer's local file system to a target drop area in the interface. Most to-do apps let you drag and drop to-do items to reorder them or move them to different lists. The more pervasive drag and drop interfaces become across the Web, the more likely people will understand how to interact with them. GitHub, for example, makes it clear that you can attach a file to a comment and that you can do this using several methods (drag and drop, select, paste). In Figure 1-9, you can see GitHub's rich text editor for comments that lets you drag and drop images.

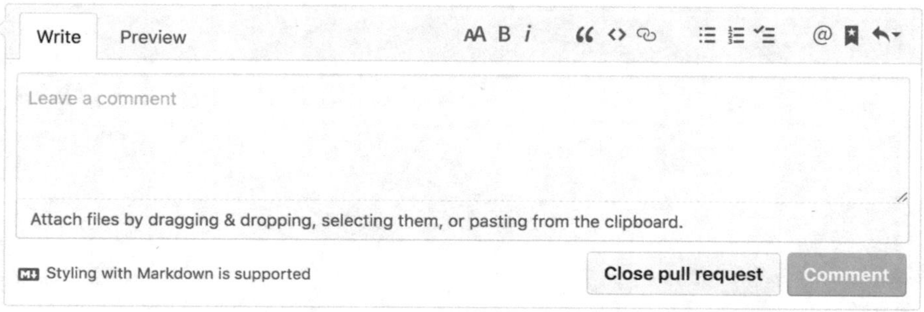

Figure 1-9. *Screenshot of GitHub's rich text editor for comments*

A text description is provided that hints at the drag behavior. Once you start dragging a file to the comment area, it is highlighted in green to reveal the drop target area, as shown in Figure 1-10.

Figure 1-10. *Screenshot of GitHub's drag and drop shows the image filename and highlights the drop target area in green*

Consistent use of patterns within a web site will help visitors build a mental model of how stuff works. If you can drag and drop files to this comment, maybe you can do that elsewhere. Sure enough, you can attach files to Pull Requests and Reviews as well, as shown in Figure 1-11.

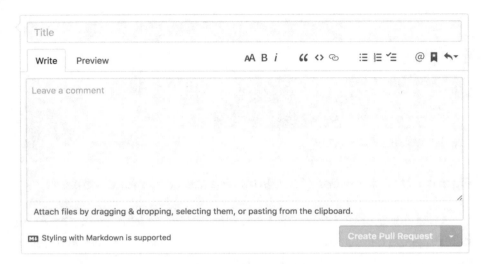

Figure 1-11. *Screenshot of GitHub's drag and drop on a Pull Request*

You can use consistency to set your visitors' expectations about how your web site works, so they may quickly learn a new area or more advanced tool by building on what they've learned already about your site.

Consistency and reuse

By their recurring nature, patterns let you reuse design solutions both visually and within code. Visual repetition lets you build consistency and predictability into your interfaces, creating a learnable experience for your users. Reusability in code also saves time, letting you refactor and improve existing features instead of rebuilding new features every time (even when something similar exists already). A pattern incorporates many design decisions to solve a problem, while programming encodes those decisions; patterns ensure you Don't Repeat Yourself (DRY), making each design decision only once. If the 548 unique colors and 261 declarations of Facebook blue (`www.lukew.com/ff/entry.asp?1469`) have taught us anything, it's to maximize reuse by minimizing inconsistency.

Communicating decisions

As a communication tool, patterns let designers persuade stakeholders and colleagues of the value of a solution. You can describe why your solution is the best for a given context. You know the purpose of a pattern, how it meets the users' needs, the similar alternatives available, and how to implement it for your brand.

Design patterns let you reference existing proven solutions, which means you have support for your decisions. Agency designers working with skeptical clients and in-house designers facing internal deadlocks sometimes need to defend specific approaches or resolve roadblocks. In these scenarios it might be useful to show how Apple use this pattern to help customers connect with customer support or Amazon used that pattern to improve conversions. This shows a concrete, tangible example of the pattern executed in the real world and helps stakeholders and colleagues visualize the desired result.

Even better than competitive contrasts, patterns can be backed by user research. Use analytics, A/B testing, user testing, customer support feedback, and survey info to show evidence for decisions. For example, "we tested this with a sample of our most engaged customers and the research shows that given the age and expertise of our visitors, the dashboard pattern works better than table filters for directing attention to desired metrics."

Further, a well-documented pattern clearly describes the user needs it meets and how it achieves that, giving you ready-made reasons to share with your stakeholders. Referring to the strengths of a pattern and consistently using patterns can relieve some of the pain points of design by committee (`www.w3.org/People/Bos/DesignGuide/committee.html`) where many people provide design input without a cohesive vision or process to resolve details, producing lower-quality work. Figure 1-12 shows a well-documented Alerts pattern.

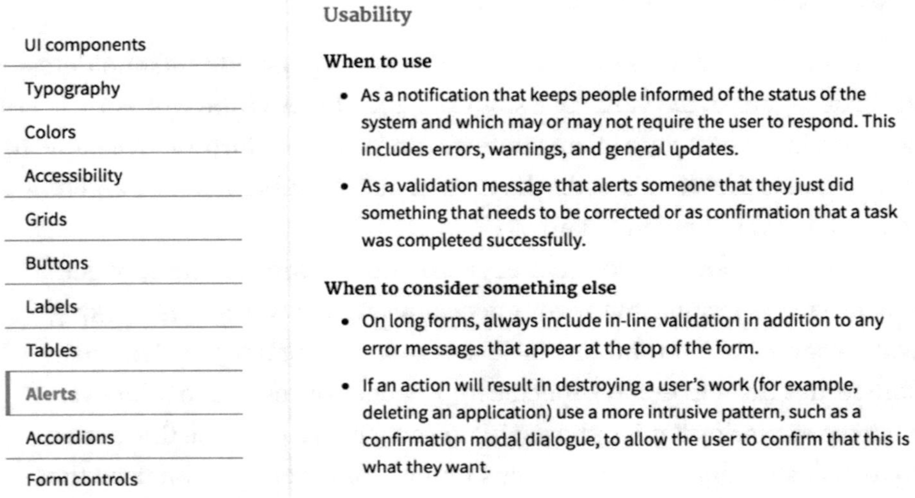

UI components	Usability

UI components

Typography

Colors

Accessibility

Grids

Buttons

Labels

Tables

Alerts

Accordions

Form controls

Usability

When to use

- As a notification that keeps people informed of the status of the system and which may or may not require the user to respond. This includes errors, warnings, and general updates.

- As a validation message that alerts someone that they just did something that needs to be corrected or as confirmation that a task was completed successfully.

When to consider something else

- On long forms, always include in-line validation in addition to any error messages that appear at the top of the form.

- If an action will result in destroying a user's work (for example, deleting an application) use a more intrusive pattern, such as a confirmation modal dialogue, to allow the user to confirm that this is what they want.

Figure 1-12. *Screenshot of U.S. Web Design Standards shows when to use Alerts components and when to consider something else*

Communicating within teams and tools

There's the joke that there are only two hard problems in computer science (https://martinfowler.com/bliki/TwoHardThings.html): cache invalidation and naming things. The joke exists because clarity through language is challenging. Evocative names speed up discussion, increase clarity, avoid mistakes, and make the underlying ideas easier to talk about. Using standard names for patterns helps designers and developers especially with talking to each other. "We might use an 'accordion menu'." "Let's test 'infinite scrolling' instead of 'pagination'." For developers, it might help to consider that CSS classes *are* patterns. Your BEM (Block, Element, Modifier) names (if you follow that convention) should describe your patterns, how they're used, and how variants are used. Similarly, increasing the use of CSS or Sass variables (https://css-tricks.com/sass-style-guide/#article-header-id-17) in your code should clarify the intent, making it easier to understand the relationships between objects (`https://thoughtbot.com/blog/sass-variables`). Figure 1-13 shows a "badge" pattern visually and in code.

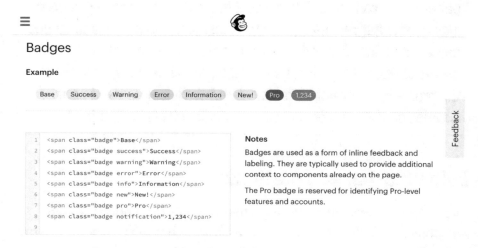

Figure 1-13. *Screenshot of MailChimp badge pattern indicates badges appear inline to provide additional context*

Note   It's worth noting that even though one benefit of patterns is that they provide a shared vocabulary for people working together across a business (including designers, developers, marketers, customers, and so on), each person interprets terms using their own background and experience, which can sometimes lead to confusion. What a marketer might call a tracking pixel or tag, a developer might call a third-party script. What a developer might call letter spacing, a designer might call tracking. What a designer might call a pixel… you see where I'm going.

In UI patterns, an autocomplete pattern might be conflated with an autosuggest pattern or described only as a "search box" or "dropdown." These discrepancies cause confusion when talking about patterns. To work around this, you'll find some patterns in this book include alternative names, with the most prominent or unambiguous name listed first. Generally, pattern names are more useful when they describe the solution, for example, "good defaults," instead of the problem, for example, "blank slate." We'll look more at pattern libraries as style guides and communication tools in Chapter 4.

Evidence-based solutions

As patterns are recurring solutions, they are only developed through repeated, successful use: if it didn't work, we shouldn't repeat it. Patterns gather up best practices and principles refined by previous designers but can also be compared with other solutions and tested with users. Patterns are also framed in terms of *how* they solve a problem. In contrast, a design principle like "give users control" is vague about how this solves problems for users. Extending our earlier thumbnail example, you can see how a collection of tiny, compressed images would be faster to download than all the high-resolution resources, so the preview collection could be perused in less time. If your images download faster, your users might stay longer. You could review your site analytics to see if their time spent on site is longer when you use thumbnails. This kind of evidence validates the success of the solution. With evidence, more people end up using the solution. This is how solutions become patterns.

You can use patterns to fast-track improvements by exploring how designers have used them before. We'll look at resources for patterns in Chapter 2.

Context-specific, tailored solutions

Patterns are context-specific. Essentially they are tailored to the precise problem. This makes them more useful than design principles (www.interaction-design.org/literature/topics/design-principles), which are excellent theories to fall back on if you need to develop a solution from scratch but are far less practical than patterns.

Content contributors without a web design background

Relying on patterns lets content contributors who are unfamiliar with the practice of web design use smart defaults. You don't always need to understand the details under the hood to get value out of existing patterns and can skip the pain of finding out the hard way that rolling your own from scratch means a lot of hard work. You can continue to specialize in your own area without sinking too much time into details.

Additionally, patterns formed by diverse contributors may be more effective and robust than, say, patterns only made by developers. More on that in Chapter 4.

Learning from the experts

Patterns let you leave the details of UI solutions to the experts in some cases and provide excellent learning material in others.

For example, by using a search filter pattern, you might be reminded to include a cancellation option to clear the filters to return to an unfiltered search, whereas designing and building search filters without reference to the pattern might leave you slowly figuring out these kinds of details one by one. Patterns let you accelerate design and development processes.

By using a standard solution, you'll be able to chat about it easily with expert communities like Stack Exchange's Stack Overflow (`https://stackoverflow.com/`) or User Experience (`https://ux.stackexchange.com/`) Q&A communities. There's also a good chance there are resources available that show patterns in action, sometimes demonstrating additional considerations. Let's consider some examples:

- Development frameworks like Bootstrap have already considered accessibility details like `role="tablist"` `aria- multiselectable="true"`.

- The Devise (`https://github.com/plataformatec/devise`) authentication solution for account registration and sign in has already considered user flow patterns like email confirmation tokens, revealing valid usernames, and more.

- Payment companies like Stripe (`https://stripe.com/`) have already considered how to balance usability and security.

In each of these cases, you can either incorporate the expert's approach into your own or dig into it further. This helps if you trust that the pattern has been executed well, but there are anti-patterns to look out for, which we'll see in Chapter 5.

Learning how to improve experiences from patterns

Patterns are a fantastic learning tool. They demonstrate reusable components that have been proven and battle-tested—you can find real examples on live sites. Patterns describe the user need that prompted its existence in the first place, for example: "Our customers are nervous about financial decisions because money is a massive stressor, so let's use reassuring words in our inline help hints, as well as live previews and confirmation patterns to improve their confidence."

They document the decisions that have been made by other designers before you. They show you the forces or factors you need to consider in your design decisions—how many size variants do we need? Contextual colors? Should alert messages be dismissable? What's the difference between a link with a button style and a button with a link style?

We'll look more at learning through patterns in Chapter 2.

Summary

A UI pattern is a recurring digital solution to a problem, in a given context. Learning and using patterns can help you

- Efficiently solve design problems across evolving interfaces as technology changes
- Produce intuitive products through consistency and familiarity
- Save time instead of repeating yourself
- Communicate design decisions
- Communicate within teams to solve problems
- Find evidence to support a solution
- Use tailored solutions for a context
- Use smart defaults without extensive product design experience
- Stand on the shoulders of giants
- Learn how to improve a user's experience

CHAPTER 2

Tap into patterns

The world is full of obvious things which nobody by any chance ever observes.

—Sherlock Holmes, *The Hound of the Baskervilles*

In this chapter we'll investigate how you can spot, and then learn, new patterns. We'll explore some tactics using a theme of signup and onboarding—everything necessary to get a new customer started and engaged.

Learning new patterns (sharpening the saw)

I suggest learning *about* patterns—which ones exist, how to find them—before learning them in depth. This lowers the learning curve and ensures that when it comes time to apply the solution, you can see it in practice, making it far more tangible and interesting to learn. At that stage you can dig deeper into the pattern and explore the intricacies of all the design decisions incorporated that you need to consider.

I consider this study sharpening the saw[1]—not to immediately solve the problem in front of you but to sharpen your saw in preparation for the real work later.

---

[1]Brett and Kate McKay, "The 7 Habits: Sharpen the Saw," www.artofmanliness.com/articles/the-7-habits-sharpen-the-saw/.

© Diana MacDonald 2019
D. MacDonald, *Practical UI Patterns for Design Systems*,
https://doi.org/10.1007/978-1-4842-4938-3_2

So, where can you hear about new patterns? I suggest browsing and skimming collections and galleries. The following types of resources can help you develop your vocabulary, identify similarities and differences in different contexts, and learn new concepts (many of them provide design principles and philosophies as well). There's a more comprehensive list in the Appendix.

Pattern collections

These are structured collections of patterns that categorize and clarify patterns. It is an extremely helpful starting point for learning what new patterns are called and the theories behind them. One modern, comprehensive collection is UI patterns (`http://ui-patterns.com/patterns/`), as shown in Figure 2-1.

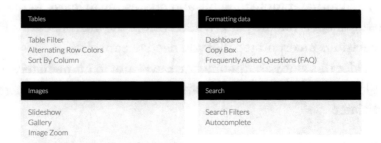

Figure 2-1. *Screenshot of UI-patterns.com design patterns dealing with data*

Pattern galleries

Pattern galleries show, rather than tell, using examples from all sorts of web sites and apps. One example is pttrns (`https://pttrns.com`), as shown in Figure 2-2.

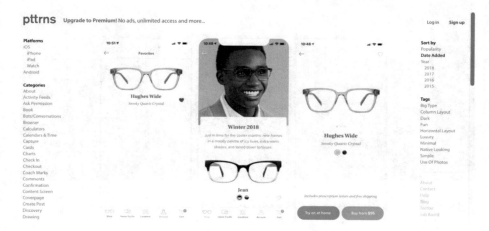

Figure 2-2.   *Screenshot of pttrns.com mobile design patterns*

There are also many domain-specific galleries that focus on a single theme, like social interfaces or e-commerce. For example, see Mobile Patterns (`www.mobile-patterns.com`) for mobile-first and native app patterns, as shown in Figure 2-3.

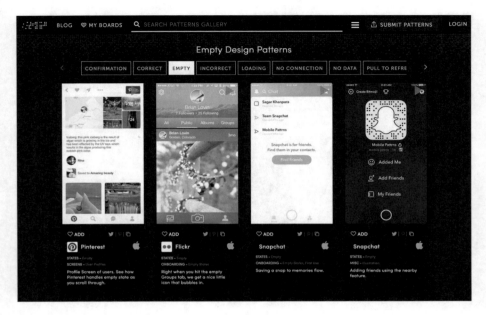

Figure 2-3. *Screenshot of Mobile Patterns*

Platform guidelines

Platform guidelines are well-tailored to the device type (mobile, laptop, wearables, etc.) and operating system (iOS, Android, Windows, etc.), more closely matching context to your needs. They're also built up from decades of improvement, refinement, and lessons learned. Consider, for example, Apple's iOS Human Interface Guidelines shown in Figure 2-4.

Make the value affected by the stepper obvious. A stepper itself doesn't display any values, so make sure people know which value they're changing when they use a stepper.

Figure 2-4. *Screenshot of Steppers in Apple developers' iOS Human Interface Guidelines*

The stepper shown in Apple's iOS guidelines is optimized for a touch device with a small screen.

As UI patterns are only relevant to a specific domain or context, these platform guidelines are only valuable insofar as they highlight the differences between platforms. Technological changes demand some push and pull, divergence and convergence, fragmentation and consolidation. We might expect movement toward cohesive cross-platform guidelines like Google's Material Design guidelines (https://material.io/design/guidelines-overview/) with more minimal guidance on platform adaptation.[2] For a striking example, the guidelines on edge swipes suggest

---

[2]Google, "Cross-platform adaptation," https://material.io/design/platform-guidance/cross-platform-adaptation.html.

27

"an edge swipe starts from outside of the screen to reveal off-screen content," and yet it might conflict with other swipe gestures, such as horizontal swipes through pages. The guidelines further describe that when there are no gesture conflicts, Android edge swipes from the left will reveal off-screen content, while iOS will navigate back through an app's hierarchy.

UI frameworks

UI patterns wouldn't be much without code to bring them to life. UI or front-end frameworks offer invaluable starting points for developers to consider the implementation of the archetypal pattern and its core elements. Designers can also use these to explore all the different "states" they need to design. Figure 2-5 shows the Tachyons (`https://tachyons.io`) framework's components section.

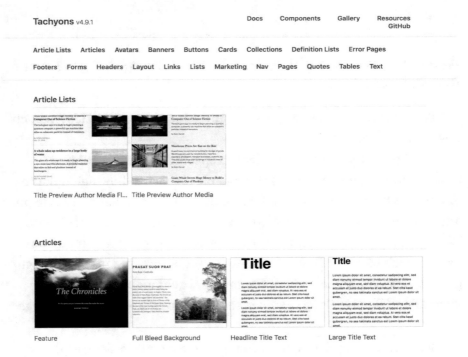

Figure 2-5. *Screenshot of Tachyons components*

Of course, you should lean on your framework if you're already using one, but sometimes you might draw from others to fill in the gaps. For example, Zurb Foundation framework[3] provides styled switch and slider components that Bootstrap does not, while Bootstrap provides inline forms that Foundation does not (at the time of writing).

Pattern libraries, design systems, style guides, and anti-patterns

Public pattern libraries and style guides from other companies and brands help demonstrate how they solved specific problems for their specific market. Design systems often include component libraries that bring patterns to life. We'll explore those further in Chapter 4. If you really want a head start, check out the Adele repository of publicly available design systems and pattern libraries (`https://adele.uxpin.com`).

Similarly, sometimes you can learn by counterexample—what not to do. Learn more in Chapter 5 on anti-patterns.

Inspiring visual style

Pattern solutions are more abstract than their exact appearance in a particular scenario, but they cannot be divorced from their visual style or real-world behavior. Visual style web sites can give you insight into the moods and trends of the design community in interpreting and remixing patterns. They provide wonderful inspiration for how a pattern may be executed to good effect. After identifying patterns that you're interested in, I suggest exploring these resources for visual style inspiration:

- Site Inspire (`www.siteinspire.com`)

- Hover States (`www.hoverstat.es`)

- Dribbble (`https://dribbble.com`)

---

[3]Zurb, "Foundation," `https://foundation.zurb.com/sites/docs/`.

Some folk are concerned about the dribbblisation of design[4]—the phenomenon of designs created to look good rather than solve real problems. I tend to believe the problem with dribbble[5] is what we make of it. It's only a platform; how we use it is up to us. It can be effective when used to test and stretch visual skills, encouraging designers to showcase and refine their visual designs as well as push the boundaries of what's possible. Being removed from the constraints of real problems might help you design an efficient and satisfying experience.[6] This can help drive innovation.

Seeing designs in action provokes you to consider cohesive experiences, seamless integration of patterns, and patterns done well. These galleries show you patterns used in award-winning designs, highly regarded within design communities:

- Awwwards (`www.awwwards.com`)

- IXDA (`http://awards.ixda.org/entries/`)

- Front-end awards (`https://thefwa.com`)

Next, we'll explore some specific patterns helpful to onboarding to give you a feel for what they look like.

Pattern: Walkthrough

A **walkthrough** is a guided tour or demo of a feature or product. It's presented in a specific order to every new user to introduce complex workflows or concepts.

---

[4]Paul Adams, "The dribbblisation of design," `https://blog.intercom.com/the-dribbblisation-of-design/`.

[5]Tobias van Schneider, "The Problem With Dribbble," `https://medium.com/%40vanschneider/the-problem-with-dribbble-8fd1627fd7d0`.

[6]For an example, see Fantasy Interactive's future of the airline case study (`http://w.fantasy-interactive.com/fi/airlines/`).

The digital product design platform, InVision, makes heavy use of walkthroughs in their products, as you can see in Figure 2-6.

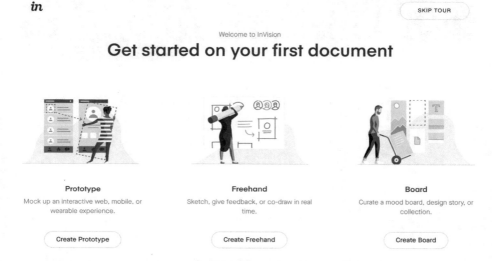

Figure 2-6. *Screenshot of InVision's walkthrough welcome*

The crux of the walkthrough pattern is to literally walk the user through each step of their core task and then to direct their focus to only one step at a time and only steps critical to completing their task.

Show the actual features or steps—for example, using screenshots—to concretely identify them in the product so the user doesn't need to remember what the feature was called and go looking for where that label might appear in the product. You needn't explore every detail of how to use a feature, but at least indicate what the important features are and how they fit within the landscape. Each step needs to instruct and inform users so they can make decisions about whether and how to use your product. Figure 2-7 shows InVision's prompt to add more screens.

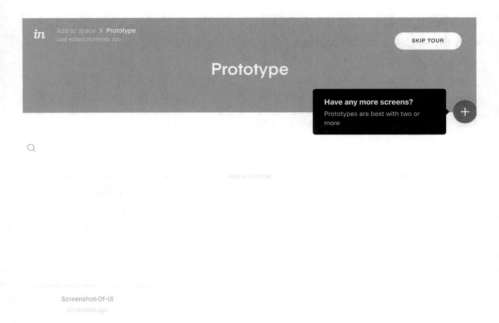

Figure 2-7. *Screenshot of InVision's walkthrough prompt to add another screen*

This walkthrough prompt lets users know that prototypes are "best with two or more" screens, encouraging them to add at least one more, while reminding them where the button is to upload and sync screens.

By letting users navigate backward and forward through a walkthrough, as well as dismiss it, they can directly access the information of most interest to them. While your user is in the walkthrough, show a progress bar or indicator to represent where they are in the process. They may wish to be assured that it's a short process containing only two more steps or otherwise keep track of which pieces of information they've seen already. For mission-critical walkthroughs that the user needs to see, such as a change in terms of use, password recovery, or recovery from a security compromise, you may need to ditch the additional navigation options.

Walkthroughs are a natural fit for first-time use. They're handy for introducing new or complex concepts or workflows, so it's important to make them available on the first page load, first site visit, first app open, and so on, considering if the user could have already seen the walkthrough on a different platform. A useful rule of thumb for when to employ a walkthrough is whenever the user may have doubts about the product.

Workflow walkthroughs

If your product is optimized for a specific workflow, introducing that workflow early on serves as signposting to help users understand how to navigate through the product and find more information when they need it. In Figure 2-8 you'll find InVision make it clear what the different modes are in their product and where they can be found, so that you can switch through the modes at your leisure later, even though they are presented in the intended order:

Figure 2-8. *Screenshot of InVision's walkthrough demo prototype project screen*

Concept walkthroughs

If your product's value proposition is disruptive and counterintuitive, use a walkthrough to break down the relevant concepts. For example, Airbnb needed to introduce their users to the share economy concept of renting out homes and apartments instead of using hotels. This brought a host of concerns for guests, such as if the place will be safe, and for hosts, such as if the property will be kept in good condition. To ease users' concerns, Airbnb needed to guide new users through the concepts with reassuring illustrations and address specific friction points, as you can see in Figure 2-9.

Safety by design

Airbnb is designed with safety—both online and off—in mind

Risk scoring

Every Airbnb reservation is scored for risk before it's confirmed. We use predictive analytics and machine learning to instantly evaluate hundreds of signals that help us flag and investigate suspicious activity before it happens.

Watchlist & background checks

While no screening system is perfect, globally we run hosts and guests against regulatory, terrorist, and sanctions watchlists. For hosts and guests in the United States, we also conduct background checks.

Preparedness

We run safety workshops with hosts and leading local experts and encourage hosts to provide guests with important local information. We also give any host who wants one a free smoke and carbon monoxide detector for their home.

Figure 2-9. *Screenshot of Airbnb's page about safety by design, showing three illustrations and supporting descriptions*

To assure guests, Airbnb describes their online and offline safety measures, including risk scoring, watchlist and background checks, and preparedness safety workshops and free smoke detectors. Similarly, you can see in Figure 2-10 how Airbnb introduces hosts to their hosting process.

Sharing your space or passions with someone you've never met can feel like a leap of faith

Here's how you can help ensure your hosting experience, and your guest's trip, goes off without a hitch

Set clear expectations

Your listing should let potential guests know about the unique features and amenities of your home or experience. Even small details like the number of flights of stairs to your front door or the fitness level required for your experience can help make sure guests enjoy their time with you.

If you're a home host, you can also outline specific expectations (like quiet hours) in your house rules.

2

Set guest requirements

Every guest is asked to provide their full name, date of birth, photo, phone number, email address, and payment information to Airbnb before booking. Home hosts also have the option to require guests to provide Airbnb with a government ID before booking their listing.

Figure 2-10. *Screenshot of Airbnb hosts, showing numbered steps with a brightly colored first step to draw attention*

Airbnb first addresses how the host might be feeling: "sharing your space or passions with someone you've never met can feel like a leap of faith." The prospective host can then see very clearly numbered steps to guide them through the process, with important explanatory details along the way.

A useful idea here is Nielsen Norman Group's mental models[7]—what users believe about a system that might differ from the designer's model. A user's beliefs will affect how they use a product, so you might use a concept walkthrough to update the user's mental model to bring it closer to how the system actually works.

---

[7]Jakob Nielsen, "Mental Models," www.nngroup.com/articles/mental-models/, October 2010.

Reserve walkthroughs for complex workflows and concepts. Instead of a walkthrough, see if you can break up the workflow further so that it's simpler and more self-explanatory, or consider a playthrough instead.

Pattern: Playthrough

A **playthrough** is an interactive tutorial or warm up that lets a user learn by doing, in a safe environment such as a sandbox.

Figure 2-11 shows an example of TeuxDeux's homepage playthrough.

Figure 2-11. *Screenshot of TeuxDeux's homepage playthrough*

TeuxDeux is a task management app. Their homepage playthrough shows a callout enticing visitors to resize the example app. The example app contains explicit instructions in its to-do items to click, hover, drag, and double-click different items, so you can "try before you buy."

When a user wants to try your product's features that are new to them, a playthrough provides a forgiving interface to let them explore safely and make mistakes without fear of repercussions. By stepping them through the product slowly, you can introduce features as needed and let them immediately play with them. There are two main scenarios for a playthrough: setup and sandbox.

Setup playthrough

Sometimes a playthrough is used as part of a setup process, for example, asking for a name, showing where it will be displayed, letting the user provide their name, then moving onto the next logical step in the product.

In Figure 2-12 you can see an empty state before the user has uploaded a cover image on their Facebook profile page.

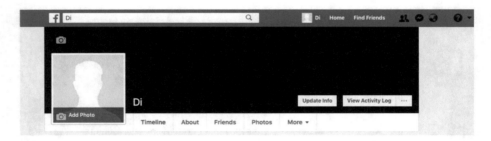

Figure 2-12. *Screenshot of Facebook profile cover image playthrough empty state*

Figure 2-13 shows an onboarding prompt to add a cover photo.

Figure 2-13. *Screenshot of Facebook profile cover image playthrough instruction*

After the user adds a cover, Figure 2-14 shows an instruction to reposition the image with a live preview of how it will look to other users.

Figure 2-14. *Screenshot of Facebook profile cover image playthrough preview and reposition*

This illustrates how a user plays through the app to set up their profile.

Sandbox playthrough

A sandbox playthrough provides sample resources with instructions on how to use them. For example, TeuxDeux starts new users with a few pre-filled tasks that teach you how to use the app, just like their homepage.

Apple's Swift Playgrounds epitomizes the playthrough pattern. It's a whole app dedicated to being a sandboxed interactive tutorial to learning Swift, as shown in Figure 2-15.

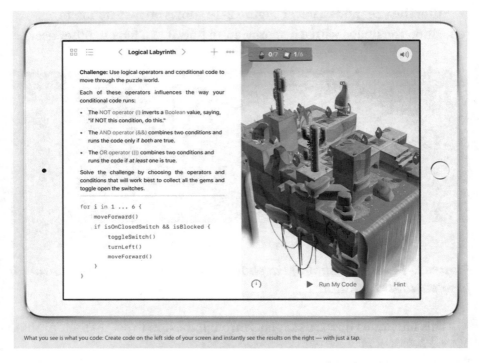

Figure 2-15. *Screenshot of Apple's Swift Playgrounds*

When to use a playthrough

Playthroughs let users immediately interact with the core tasks. This aspect in particular separates playthroughs from walkthroughs, demos, and other instructional content. It's an excellent opportunity to demonstrate the value of the feature without delay. Likewise, interactivity can improve the learning experience, so it feels easy.

Using this pattern to provide a sandbox can be handy when your product's user wants to avoid "breaking real data." For example, see InVision's Freehand tutorial in Figure 2-16.

Add text

Click where you'd like to add text (T). Type "User Name".

Figure 2-16. *Screenshot of InVision's Freehand tutorial with a pending instruction*

This lets people draw with wild abandon. They may be free from concern of losing their own work by trying out new Freehand features in the tutorial. You can see the user has an opportunity to ask for help to complete the step if they want to move on.

Once the user has completed the step (tried the feature), they're given an option to move to the next step, as shown in Figure 2-17.

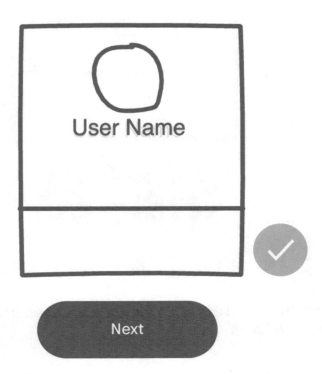

Figure 2-17. *Screenshot of InVision's Freehand tutorial with a successful step done*

As with Walkthroughs, some people might want to navigate through your product via unexpected paths, so consider if you need to show an easy exit, such as a "Skip all" link or links to navigate backward through previous steps. In InVision's Freehand example, there's an option on every step to "Skip tutorial," and on every Freehand, there's an option to "Review tutorial."

After a new user has played through your product's features, make it easy to take off the training wheels. They've learned what they need to know, so provide an easy method to remove any unwanted sample data. It can be frustrating to find that sample data contributes to account limits, like the number of projects you're allowed to have before upgrading. In InVision's Freehand example, the tutorial lets the user play without creating a Freehand that could clutter up their account.

This pattern demonstrates how the context of the user's place in their journey drastically changes the relevance of the pattern. If they were an expert user, these playthrough experiences might be infuriating. This is a reminder that patterns are solutions to problems *in a context*.

Playthroughs can be overkill when the consequences of exploring unguided are minimal. Avoid them if users can make trivial mistakes and recover from them without guidance. For example, the consequences of searching for the "wrong" term in a search function might result in useless results, but the user can easily type in a new search term—no guidance is needed.

Pattern: Newsletter signup

A **newsletter signup** is a form that allows users to subscribe to a list. They may then be sent email news about the product to keep them informed about regularly changing content.

Figure 2-18 shows an example of a newsletter signup.

Figure 2-18. *Screenshot of Web Animation Weekly signup*

There are strong conventions across the Web for email newsletter signup forms. Let's look at their key elements.

> **Label**: Most newsletters provide an explicit "Email Address" `label` element to identify the component. Sometimes, it implied through a call to action. For example, on the newsletter signup section on the Bellroy web site for carry goods, there is the line: "Being In The Know Feels Great: Signup here for news and updates," which you can see in Figure 2-19.

Figure 2-19. *Screenshot of Bellroy newsletter signup*

> **Input**: Your visitor needs somewhere to provide an email address. In code, this is generally a standard HTML `input` element. It's also common to use the attribute `type="email"` to ensure the correct keyboard appears on mobile devices (one that shows an "@" symbol to make it easy to type the email address) and to assist browser autofill behavior.

> **Submit button**: Your visitor also needs a means of confirming and sending the email address when they're finished typing. For example, you could use a submit button, press the Return/Enter key on a keyboard, or tap the "Go" button on mobile devices.

"Submit" can be a jargon term though, so consider another label for your button that describes the action being taken, such as "Signup."

List: When your visitor subscribes to your newsletter, you'll need to add their email address to a list. This might seem obvious enough, but what happens next can vary wildly. Many email service providers will automatically send a "double opt-in" confirmation email to your visitor's email address that they must confirm before being permanently added to the list. In another scenario, if it's a manually collected and stored list, you'll need to know how to pull this list of email addresses later into your email service provider app when it comes time to send your newsletter.

Validation: You'll likely want to validate the email address input provided to you. For example, it is common to reject email addresses without an "@" symbol. Many products use a CAPTCHA (Completely Automated Public Turing test to tell Computers and Humans Apart) to weed out bots and other fake signups by presenting a test that is easy for a human and challenging for a computer to answer.[8] You can learn more about form validation in the validation feedback section ahead. For a deeper look at forms, I recommend the book, *Designing UX: Forms* by Jessica Enders.

---

[8]CAPTCHAs www.usertesting.com/blog/2014/04/09/think-your-site-needs-captcha-try-these-user-friendly-alternatives/.

Legal: When providing personal information, your users need to know how their information will be used. Either provide details inline or a link to further information about your privacy policy or terms and conditions. Critically, ensure your users know exactly what they are signing up for. When signing up for a free O'Reilly ebook, you're also given an optional checkbox to subscribe to their newsletter while the button says "Get the free ebook," so you know exactly what to expect. You can also follow the link "We protect your privacy," to see the privacy policy, shown in Figure 2-20.

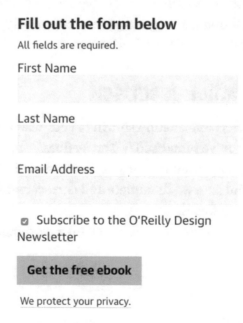

Figure 2-20. *Screenshot of O'Reilly Design Newsletter*

Use the newsletter signup pattern the first time a user wants to access email news. If they've already subscribed to your newsletter, avoid using this pattern. You can check if they've already subscribed before showing the signup form by examining their user account (if they are logged in) or by seeing if they have just come to your site by your newsletter. You can do this by or looking at the URL in the address bar (or in code by inspecting the HTML referer path[9]) to see if it includes tracking links from your newsletter such as `/?utm_medium=email&utm_campaign=newsletter`. If a visitor comes from your newsletter, don't show the signup form.

Another time to avoid this pattern is if user's email address is not subscribed to the newsletter list, but you already have their address for other reasons (such as account login). In this case, you could show an opt-in checkbox instead of asking them to type in their address again.

Let's see another first-time signup pattern commonly seen with newsletter subscription: validation feedback.

Pattern: Validation feedback

Validation feedback is information shown to your user after they've provided data and you've processed it. The feedback might be a warning or suggestion, an error preventing further progress until it's been fixed, or confirmation that the data was complete and correct. Validation feedback most often appears on forms.

Figure 2-21 shows validation feedback with a *warning*.

---

[9]Wikipedia, "HTTP referer," `https://en.wikipedia.org/wiki/HTTP_referer`.

Figure 2-21. Screenshot of a newsletter warning validation feedback

This example suggests the "Email address should follow the format user@domain.com." Often a validation warning lets the user continue at their own peril.

Figure 2-22 shows validation feedback with an *error*.

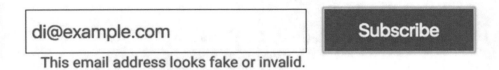

Figure 2-22. *Screenshot of a newsletter warning with an error*

This example shows the error message: "This email address looks fake or invalid. Please enter a real email address." Usually an error prevents any further progress until it's been corrected.

Figure 2-23 shows validation feedback indicating a soft *confirmation*.

Thank you!

You will receive a
request to confirm
your subscription.

Figure 2-23. *Screenshot of successful subscription*

This example says, "Thank you! You will receive a request to confirm your subscription.", encouraging further action to be taken to finish the process.

Finally, Figure 2-24 shows validation feedback indicating *confirmation* of a successfully completed process.

Figure 2-24. *Screenshot of Atlassian's confirmation message*

This kind of validation feedback assures the user that their work is done and celebrates the effort they've put in.

Validating user input and providing feedback about it give them an opportunity to correct the input. If it's likely you'll receive incomplete or incorrect information that is needed for your visitor to use your product, help them recover using this pattern.

To prevent exasperating your users, clarify the validation rules they need to meet in order to complete the process, so they don't need to figure them out by trial and error. One method to do this is to provide a tailored message for each validation rule that affects the user. For each message

1. Use plain language, front-load keywords, and omit needless words.

2. Indicate any problems using concrete, specific, and precise nouns.

3. Suggest next steps or solutions using positive, active verbs.

Another convenient method to assist your user is to preserve all their input during and after validation. Imagine your user says their date of birth is a date in the future yet to pass. You might be tempted to validate the date of birth against the current date, show feedback that the provided date is in the future and therefore needs to be changed, and clear the provided date, asking them to type in a new one. It is likely easier, however, for your user to adjust the year by one digit from 2091 to 2001 than to start all over again filling out the day, month, and year. Preserve their data. You might then draw attention to which part is incorrect by highlighting the year visually and providing a specific message to review the year.

Use the validation feedback pattern when it's important to you to have accurate data. For a newsletter, having a lot of fake signups on your list can be costly if you are paying an email service provider per email address.

Using the validation feedback pattern lets you increase the user's confidence that they've taken the right action (positive feedback) or help them recover from errors (negative feedback). For clarity, provide your feedback as close in proximity and time as possible to the action the user took.

In addition to warnings, errors, and confirmations, one underappreciated form of feedback is a gentle suggestion that hints at better steps rather than prevents further progress. One instance where it can help is inspecting phone numbers. Validating international phone numbers is a notoriously difficult task due to the wild variation in acceptable formats globally as well as how people format their numbers when they provide them. When asking for an optional phone number, you might include a validation warning or suggestion when the user provides a number that looks like it might be wrong, encouraging the visitor to check it, but avoid showing a validation error that prevents task completion. The visitor can then proceed with a fake or badly formatted phone number, but you've prompted them to check it twice for their own benefit. For example, consider this message:

Enter your phone number to help fast delivery of your order.

Identifying relevant patterns

You can identify further relevant patterns in addition to this book using a few jump-off points:

- In a collection, look at patterns in the same category.

- In a pattern, look at "Related patterns."

- Competitive analysis (more on that ahead).

One more is good ol' fashioned brainstorming. Starting with one pattern, snowball your way to other relevant solutions. One time I faced an unusual design problem: radiologists wanted to see patient case imaging results on a web site. They needed to see a specific medical condition across a stack of images (e.g., a CT scan of a brain with a stack of images showing the brain at different slices with different parts of the tumor present in each slice). While this might look like an unusual and complex UI problem, even here we can find relevant ideas to inform us:

- Image viewing

- Image editing

- Image annotation

- Map annotation

- Map regions

- Videos

- Video annotation

- Flick books

In this way, I found some existing "best practices" for a seemingly new issue.

Useful patterns describe how they solve the problem, including salient details on why it works the way it does. These patterns can inform you even when the problem is actually slightly different.

This is how patterns may actually foster creativity—remixing existing solutions for new problems—rather than constrain creativity as they are sometimes blamed for doing.

Searching for patterns

The resources in this chapter highlight many available patterns to use. It's helpful to see them in large collections like these, with similar patterns side by side, but sometimes specific patterns for unusual areas are harder to find. For example, admin interfaces pose their own interesting challenges. While UI patterns might have taught you about the existence of table filters, sort by column, and search filters, it may be challenging to bring all those patterns together effectively, and they're far from comprehensive.

A quick Internet search for "Admin design patterns" reveals Magento's excellent Admin Design Pattern Library (`https://devdocs.magento.com/guides/v2.3/pattern-library/bk-pattern.html`). They also include a signup form pattern that highlights the different states the form can be in—initial, error, password retrieval, confirmation of password retrieval, error of password retrieval, and successful sign out. As a designer, this suggests all the different mockups you might need to assemble. As a developer, this suggests all the validation types required and possible states an account can be in. You can see this example in Figure 2-25.

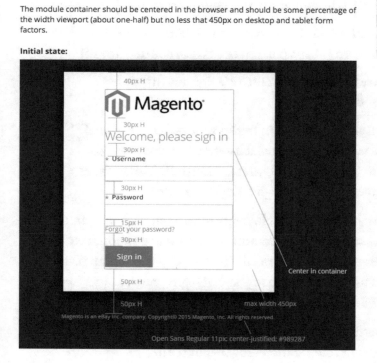

Figure 2-25. *Screenshot of Magento signup form initial state style*

By knowing the standard and alternative names of many patterns, you can find interesting information about patterns. Outside of "patterns," you might add "UX" or "best practices" to your search queries to find more design considerations to explore. By having the vocabulary, you can ask concise questions about a pattern.

Let's see some examples of discovering and learning new patterns using the resources and techniques in this book.

Pattern: Social signup

Let's say you've perused the pattern collections and found mention of a social login in UI pattern's account registration pattern.[10] To learn more about it, you might search for more information. To demonstrate, using the resources included in the Appendix you could discover

- A detailed social signup pattern in UIPatterns.io's social login pattern (`http://uipatterns.io/social-login`)

- Real-world examples in Pttrns's signups (`https://pttrns.com/?scid=9`)

- A social signup pattern in the specific domain of social interfaces: Designing Social Interfaces' Signup or Registration pattern (`www.designingsocialinterfaces.com/patterns/Sign_Up_or_Registration`)

From here, we learn that a **social signup pattern** uses integration with a visitor's existing social media accounts to signup to a product without creating a new username or password, fast-tracking the signup process.

Digging even further, a search for "social login pattern" and "social signup pattern" finds these additional useful resources:

- Mobiscroll: Social login pattern (`https://blog.mobiscroll.com/social-login-pattern/`)

- Nic Werner's Product Pattern: Social login (`https://medium.com/product-labs/product-pattern-social-login-3b50eb7e8db3#.oxs34buo3`)

- Six Revisions: A Guide to Social Logins (`http://sixrevisions.com/web-development/social-logins/`)

---

[10]UI-Patterns, "Account Registration," `http://ui-patterns.com/patterns/AccountRegistration`.

Now we know a good deal about social signups. As we progress through the book, we'll learn more about how to put patterns like this into practice.

Pattern: Lazy signup

Suppose you've also browsed the pattern collections and discovered the lazy signup pattern (`http://ui-patterns.com/patterns/LazyRegistration`) in UI pattern's account registration pattern that lets visitors "access a limited set of features, functionality, or content before or without registering." Here you learn it's also called immediate immersion or gradual engagement. From UIPatterns.io's lazy signup pattern (`http://uipatterns.io/lazy-signup`), we learn that while this user flow pattern suggests delaying the account registration or signup process, once that becomes necessary, you can use the social signup or simple account registration pattern. Using the pattern resources listed in the Appendix to explore further, we can find

- Real-world examples in UXArchive's signing up tasks (`http://uxarchive.com/tasks/signing_up`)

- A social signup pattern in the specific domain of social interfaces: Designing Social Interfaces' Signup or Registration pattern (`www.designingsocialinterfaces.com/patterns/Sign_Up_or_Registration`)

- Mobile-specific signup patterns in mobile patterns signup flows (`www.mobile-patterns.com/search/patterns?q=sign-up-flows%3Asubtags`)

- Code example in Tachyons (`http://tachyons.io/components/forms/sign-up/index.html`)

- Code samples and examples under the "Signup" tag in Zurb's pattern tap and building blocks library (https://zurb.com/library/)

- Delightful signup examples in LittleBigDetails (http://littlebigdetails.com/search/signup)

A search for "Gradual engagement" also reveals these handy articles:

- UXBooth's lesson in gradual engagement (www.uxbooth.com/articles/a-lesson-in-gradual-engagement/).

- Luke Wroblewski on A List Apart talks about gradual engagement in Signup Forms Must Die (https://alistapart.com/article/signupforms).

I'd also suggest exploring other onboarding patterns,[11] such as paywalls/signup walls. Something outside your initial ideas might be just right for your needs.

Great, now we know what a signup might look like and the kinds of design decisions we need to make. Next, let's explore competitive analysis and learning from the best.

Competitive analysis

Continuing our research into patterns in the real world, we've reviewed successful visual concepts for patterns. It's also useful to review patterns through the lens of business viability. Seeing patterns implemented by highly successful companies can give you extra reassurance that you're on the right track. Likewise finding missed opportunities by your competitors can set your designs apart.

---

[11]UI-Patterns, "Onboarding," http://ui-patterns.com/patterns/onboarding/list.

A solid place to start is by reviewing your direct competitors. Read your competitors' customer reviews, support forums, and social media. Frequently you'll find gripes about a product interface that highlight failed solutions, which can indicate

- A custom solution or "innovation" where an existing pattern could work better

- Poorly selected patterns, ineffective for the problem at hand

- Poorly executed patterns, deviating from effective pattern usage

Sometimes you'll find delighted comments on ease of use, showing where a pattern has worked effectively.

Beyond your direct competitors, you can find useful research sources among indirect competitors:

- Largest Internet companies

- Largest tech companies

- Fortune 500 companies by revenue

- Alexa top 500 sites on the Web by traffic

- Industry leaders in your vertical market

- The best web sites in your space: informational / e-commerce / NGO or non-profit / government / social

Seeing patterns used by larger brands also reveals some evidence that the solution has worked on a meaningful scale.

Learn from the best

When improving your skills, it's best to draw guidance from the experts—both for learning efficient methods of achieving effective results and for gaining feedback on your own progress. When deconstructing a new skill[12] you want to learn, interviewing an expert or reversing an expert's final results lets you break down complex solutions into manageable pieces to study. Once you have a pattern you'd like to learn more about, see if there's a specialist that can teach you more.

There are experts in specific niches that can help with particular qualities of the pattern your working on, such as Medium for reading experiences and typography[13] or Apple for design-centric products and web sites (pro-tip: they do localization well too).

More broadly, you can also learn from experts in related industries that have a longer history than modern web and product design. Here are some examples:

- Animation, cinema, entertainment for motion design

- Editorial magazines for blogs

- Journals for article content sites

- Stock market for displaying real-time data

- Information architecture for navigation and search

Seek inspiration outside your own circles whenever you can. This provides diverse perspectives, resulting in stronger designs.

Let's see some examples of how to bring patterns to life in your product.

---

[12]Richard Feloni, "Tim Ferriss explains how the 'DiSSS' system can be used to learn any skill," `www.businessinsider.com.au/tim-ferriss-disss-system-to-learn-anything-2015-3`, March 2015.

[13]Marcin Wichary, "Death to typewriters," `https://medium.design/death-to-typewriters-9b7712847639#.q55st6v5w`, February 2015.

Pattern: Notifications

A **notification** is a message object that presents timely information, including alerts, errors, reminders, cookie warnings, and requests.

When you need to provide time-sensitive, contextual information to a user, use a notification that appears close to the user's point of focus or current task.

Figure 2-26 shows an example of a notification.

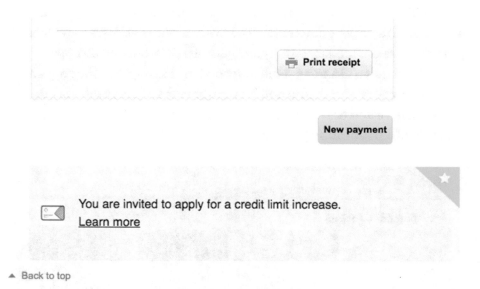

Figure 2-26. Screenshot of Commonwealth Bank's post-task upsell notification

In this example, the Commonwealth Bank of Australia shows an upsell notification immediately after finishing a related task (making a payment) and immediately below that task.

An important design decision for notifications is whether and how it can be dismissed. A simple rule of thumb is asking yourself, "If the user dismisses the notification, does the page still make sense?" For example,

Semantic UI's Nag (`https://semantic-ui.com/modules/nag.html`) notifications "are used to present a user with a one-time message which will persist until a user acknowledges the message. This can be used for providing notices like the site's use of cookies, an important change to a site like a security breach." In this case, you'll need to make a note somewhere in your system when they've acknowledged and dismissed the notification, in a cookie, session, or user account records. Then don't show the notification again.

Another consideration is if you'll need consecutive notifications and if they should fade away automatically. For example, snackbars[14] and toasts[15] provide transient messages that automatically time out and disappear. Only one is ever shown at a time, removing previous messages as they appear.

Furthermore, should the notification appear the next time the page or screen is visited or when the user next logs in? Figure 2-27 shows an example of a notification presented when a user logs in.

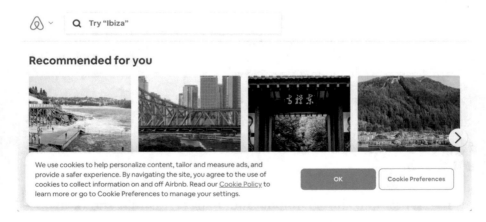

Figure 2-27. *Screenshot of Airbnb's cookie notification*

---

[14]Google, "Snackbars," `https://material.io/design/components/snackbars.html`.

[15]Yan Zhu, "Toasts - Components - Spectre.css CSS Framework," `https://picturepan2.github.io/spectre/components/toasts.html`.

This notification informs the user how cookies are used, what the user is agreeing to, and where to learn more or manage "Cookie Preferences."

Containers for notifications

When presenting a notification, you'll likely need to pair it with a content container pattern.

For a task-specific notification, consider an inline panel, such as Foundation's Callout[16] or Bootstrap's Alert,[17] immediately next to the task itself. Figure 2-28 shows an inline panel related to the task that was just completed.

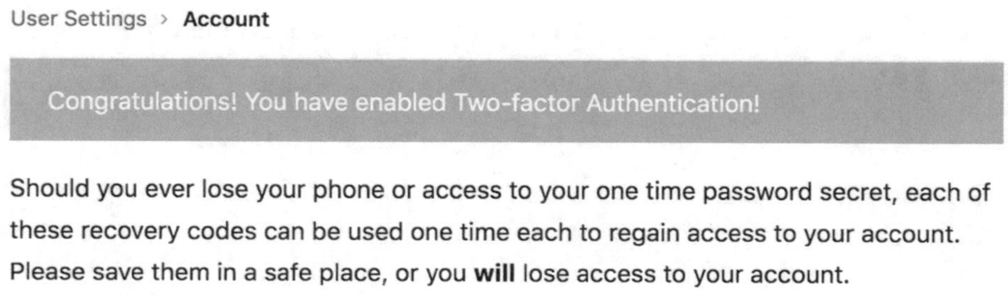

User Settings › **Account**

Congratulations! You have enabled Two-factor Authentication!

Should you ever lose your phone or access to your one time password secret, each of these recovery codes can be used one time each to regain access to your account. Please save them in a safe place, or you **will** lose access to your account.

Figure 2-28. *Screenshot of GitLab's task-related notification*

For messages that extend to the entire system or are likely to stick around after returning to a page or screen, use overarching screen elements, such as Foundation's Sticky navigation[18] or Bootstrap's fixed Navbar.[19] Figure 2-29 shows a fixed notification at the top of the page.

---

[16]Zurb, "Callout," http://foundation.zurb.com/sites/docs/callout.html.

[17]Bootstrap, "Alerts," http://getbootstrap.com/components/#alerts.

[18]Zurb, "Sticky," http://foundation.zurb.com/sites/docs/sticky.html.

[19]Bootstrap, "Navbar placement," https://getbootstrap.com/docs/4.3/components/navbar/#placement.

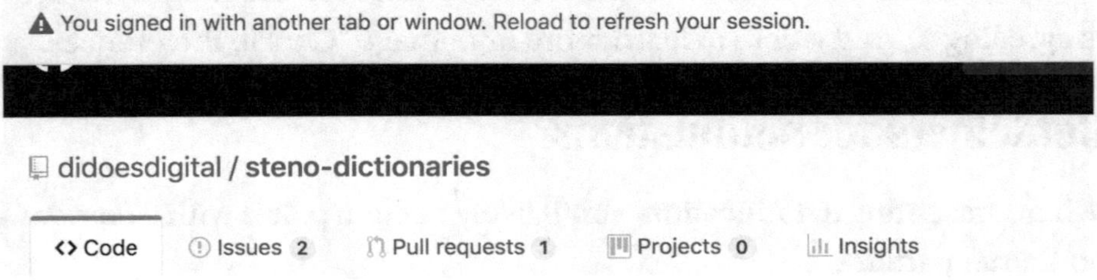

⚠ You signed in with another tab or window. Reload to refresh your session.

🖵 didoesdigital / **steno-dictionaries**

‹› Code   ⓘ Issues **2**   ⌥ Pull requests **1**   ▥ Projects **0**   ▦ Insights

Figure 2-29.   Screenshot of GitHub's reload session banner

When triggering an alert according to some user action like logging in after an extended period, try overlay components, such as Spectre's modal,[20] Semantic UI's dimmer,[21] Bootstrap's popover,[22] or Foundation's tooltip.[23] Figure 2-30 shows a modal containing a notification after logging in.

---

[20]Yan Zhu, "Modals - Components - Spectre.css CSS Framework," `https://picturepan2.github.io/spectre/components.html#modals`.

[21]Semantic UI, "Dimmer," `https://semantic-ui.com/modules/dimmer.html`.

[22]Bootstrap, "Popovers," `http://getbootstrap.com/javascript/#popovers`.

[23]Zurb, "Tooltip," `http://foundation.zurb.com/sites/docs/tooltip.html`.

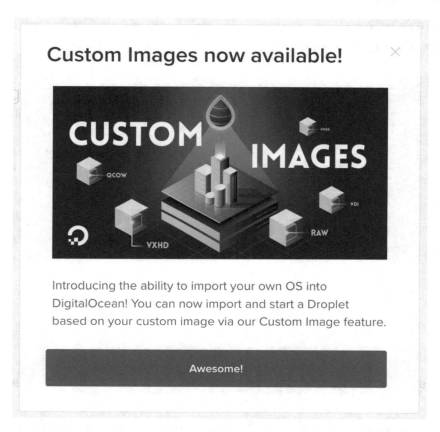

Figure 2-30. *Screenshot of Digital Ocean's new feature notification for returning visitor*

Using one visual style for all of your notifications lets you establish a cohesive and predictable experience for your customers or visitors. On the other hand, adapting notifications to more precisely fit in close proximity to their trigger can provide more clarity. When a notification appears near the action that triggered it, the relationship is clear, and the user can figure out what steps to take next. The value of these trade-offs varies—as you might expect—by product or web site.

If there's complex information needed to understand or resolve the notification, include links to further information or a reference of where to find this information in the future. Figure 2-31 shows an error that might be confusing to some people.

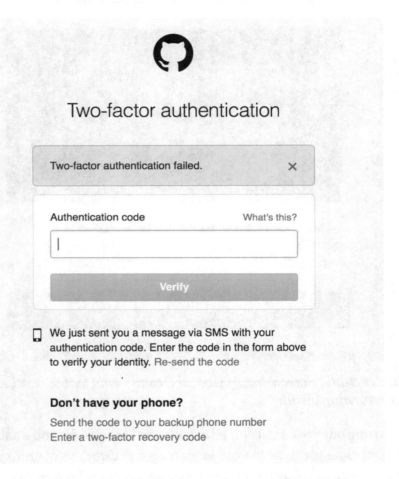

Figure 2-31. *Screenshot of GitHub's two-factor authentication with error*

Next to the form field, there's a link labeled "What's this?" to learn more, as well as supplementary text below the form elaborating on how to find the data needed to enter into the form and proceed.

In most cases, you'll want to include a clear call to action in your notification, such as a button to acknowledge the message ("Got it!"), a button to enable permissions ("Turn on notifications"), or a link to a task to take further action ("Go to Your Account Settings").

The opportune moment

When making a request to enable permissions, wait until the user has requested the feature that needs extra permissions. This is an example of the Kairo pattern of waiting until the opportune moment to communicate, so that you improve the chances of your user making the change you want.[24] In contrast, requesting desktop notifications for a first-time visitor to your site before they've read any of your content is unlikely to succeed compared to asking after they've read and shared your content.

Notifications are best used for short, time-sensitive messages. Don't use them when inline copy would be better, or the message can wait until a better moment.

Using what we've learned so far and the pattern resources in the Appendix, we can quickly find some notifications in action:

- FWA's Outside case study (https://thefwa.com/cases/outside) shows setting a push notification for weather forecasts.

- Andrew McKay's Atlassian notifications illustration animation (https://dribbble.com/shots/2518631-Notifications-Illustration-Animation) shows an animation for Atlassian's notification to "turn on notifications" for first use.

---

[24]UI-Patterns, "Kairos," http://ui-patterns.com/patterns/Kairos.

Pattern: Good defaults

Good defaults for any information a user might need to provide can make it easier or faster for the user to provide it.

Figure 2-32 shows an example of replying to a message using a single button tap of one of three possible pre-canned messages, taking the hard work out of composing a response.

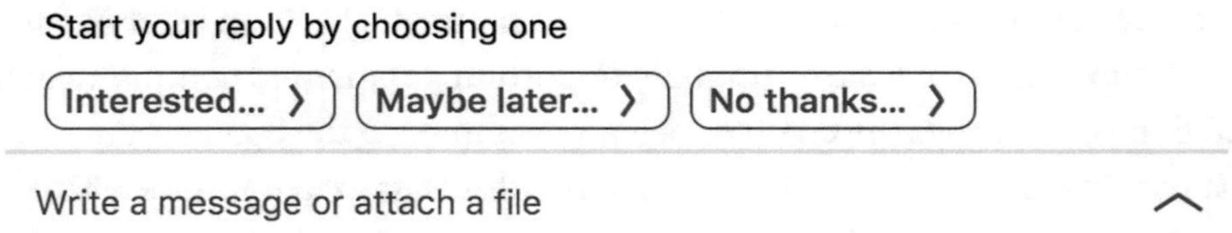

Start your reply by choosing one

(Interested... 〉) (Maybe later... 〉) (No thanks... 〉)

Write a message or attach a file   ⌃

Figure 2-32. *Screenshot of LinkedIn's good defaults*

For onboarding new users to an interface, use good defaults that demonstrate value, like delighting users with examples of the most common use case for the product. For example, a photo sharing site could use selfies. Similarly, to avoid boring empty states for new users, use placeholders that illustrate how the interface might look after the user refines it with their personalized choices. One option is to pre-fill applications with sample items and guide the user on how to interact with them as we saw in playthroughs.

Good defaults require some understanding of what data has a better than even chance of being selected, so user research is important here. You might use defaults chosen from data provided by the majority of existing users to pre-fill empty fields. In other cases, you could pre-fill empty fields using existing data known about the current user, such as their location (determined using IP address), screen size, time they are using the site, and so on.

To use good defaults effectively, it's useful to support

- Browser or device autofill by using the correct HTML `labels` and `input types`

- Password managers for their own autofill behavior as well as password generation

- Filling out profiles using existing info from elsewhere such as importing contacts from other address books

Good defaults are especially helpful when a new user has empty data sets or other empty states—avoid blank slates that paralyze users with ambiguity because they don't know where to start.

You can also use good defaults when requesting information, including for any form, to make the process of providing information faster. Balance this with the tendency for people to skip fields that look complete already. You could do this by asking for confirmation or visually treating it as incomplete. Skip using good defaults completely if there are negative consequences for a field being incorrect and overlooked. For example, a phone case size selector could default to "iPhone X" because it's the most popular choice, but the user still needs to consciously choose the correct size to match their phone or risk costly returns processes when receiving the wrong case.

Pattern: Coachmarks

A **coachmark** is instructional overlay content placed close to new features to help new users learn difficult interfaces.

For example, see Pinterest's first-use animated coachmarks, shown in Figure 2-33.

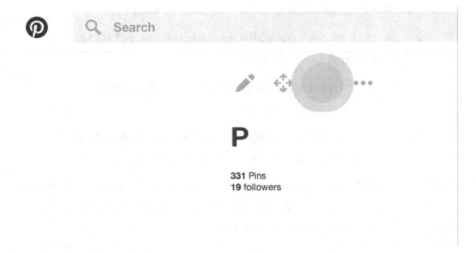

Figure 2-33. *Screenshot of Pinterest's animated coachmarks*

Pinterest would highlight new features in blue until the user had tried them, as you can see in Figure 2-34.

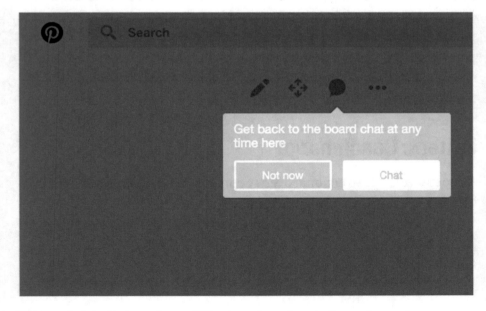

Figure 2-34. *Screenshot of Pinterest's animated coachmarks*

This uses motion to draw your attention and a blue outline to highlight its newness, separating it from other, existing features. This style goes away as soon as you've acknowledged the feature.

To use coachmarks effectively, show tiny snippets of microcopy near important features to draw user's attention and explain and visually indicate the "modality"—that is, indicate whether or not interaction with the coached feature will be impeded by the coachmark until you've dismissed it. You can use a transparent overlay over the rest of the page. You might consider automatically dismissing the coachmark when the user is interacting with the page. Figure 2-35 shows an example of how LinkedIn introduced people to the Enter key behavior in messages using a coachmark.

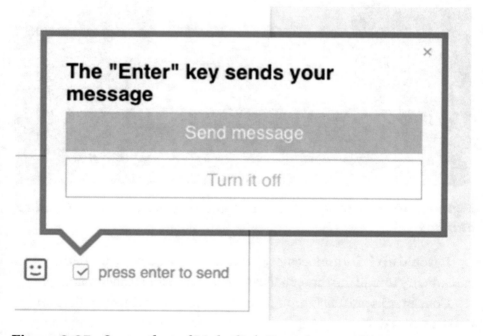

Figure 2-35. Screenshot of LinkedIn's Enter key notification

Because coachmarks draw attention, use them in moderation (don't fill the page with coachmarks). Only use them when new users need assistance but providing the content inline would hamper the majority usage by return users. Figure 2-36 shows an example of a coachmark for introducing a new feature that only needs to be explained once.

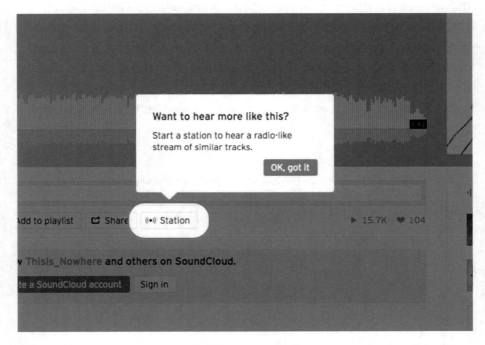

Figure 2-36. *Screenshot of SoundCloud use coachmarks to introduce Stations*

It would likely be unnecessary to clutter the interface with that explanatory text all the time, so it can be reserved for a coachmark.

Coachmarks and walkthroughs can be tricky. Imagine installing an app on a new device, logging into the same account as usual, and being forced through a lengthy collection of coachmarks explaining features you've used a thousand times before you can use them again. This is an opportunity for interface reduction. For any user account notifications, record the user's acknowledgment of the message when they dismiss it, and never show it again. Figure 2-37 shows a notification that would be superfluous for many repeat visitors.

Figure 2-37. *Screenshot of ListenOnRepeat's coachmark lets visitors know they can search without interrupting their current video*

Implementing and tailoring patterns

After learning new patterns, clarifying your design problem, and identifying patterns relevant to your interests, how might you tailor a pattern precisely to your needs? It's not enough to name the solution to your problem in the given context; you need to flesh out all the implementation details. Many patterns will describe the list of things you need to think about (see Chapter 1). It's also important to use your own user research—like the user journeys and personas we'll look at in Chapter 3. Sometimes, you'll need to specify how the pattern is implemented and how it might vary across *your* product—learn more in Chapter 4. Sometimes you'll need to avoid them turning into anti-patterns—see Chapter 5. Finally, see Chapter 6 to string them altogether in your product.

One important thing is that you do user research. Test. Prototype. Test some more.

Pattern: Progressive disclosure

A previous version of Apple's MacOS Human Interface Guidelines defined Apple's "User Control" design principle as "The principle of user control presumes that the user, not the computer, should initiate and control actions." Further, Apple described **progressive disclosure** as "hiding additional information or more complex UI until the user needs or requests it" to "help you provide the right level of user control."[25]

For example, see MailChimp's disclosure element (`https://ux.mailchimp.com/patterns/forms#disclosure`) shown in Figure 2-38.

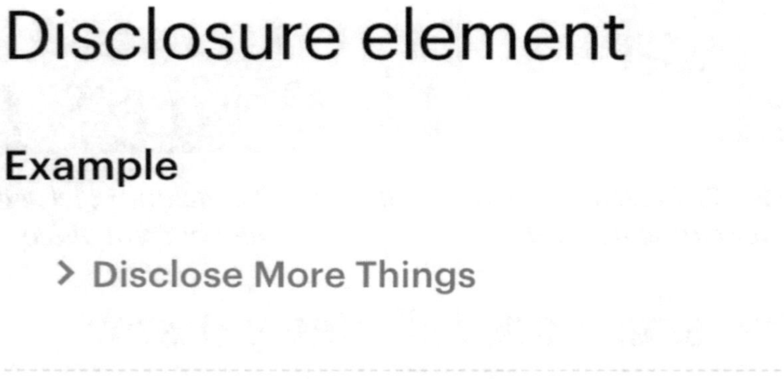

Disclosure element

Example

> Disclose More Things

Figure 2-38. *Screenshot of MailChimp's disclosure element*

To progressively disclose information, hide the extended information by default and provide a trigger that lets the user activate visibility of the hidden content, such as a link. After activation, bring more content into view in direct proportion to the user's desire for more content.

---

[25]Apple, "Design Principles," `http://web.archive.org/web/20161012234942/` `https://developer.apple.com/library/content/documentation/` `UserExperience/Conceptual/OSXHIGuidelines/DesignPrinciples.html`.

Use progressive disclosure when most users do not need all the information and some users will need more information at some point in time.

Many common user interface components incorporate this technique by default, including

- Accordions

- Tooltips

- "View all" links (e.g., on comment threads or product ranges)

- Read more links for inline content expansion

Pattern: Staged disclosure

Similar to progressive disclosure, *staged disclosure* presents additional information in steps (or stages) according to the user's direct request. In contrast, however, staged disclosure refers to a linear flow tunneling through a larger process. It advances the distance through a process rather than the depth into optional information.

For example, see Apple's iPhone 8 product selection flow that provides three steps—choosing model, finish, and capacity shown in Figure 2-39.

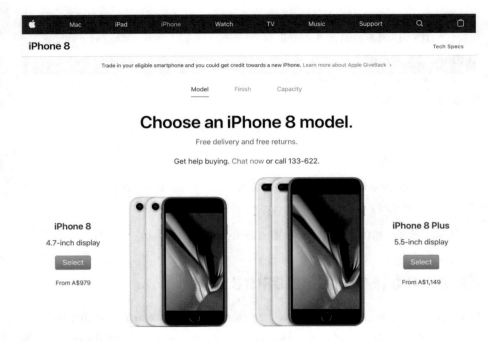

Figure 2-39. *Screenshot of Apple's multistep process*

This pattern is commonly used in signup, setup, purchase flows, and workflows.

To stage disclosure of information, chunk extended information into smaller, logical groups and present one at a time. Similar to progressive disclosure, provide a trigger to navigate to the next step, but also back links as needed, and consider pairing staged disclosure with a progress indicator.

Use staged disclosure when providing all the information at once would be overwhelming—focus users on one task or piece of information at a time.

Figures 2-40 to 2-44 show Dropbox's staged disclosure for introducing two-factor authentication concepts.

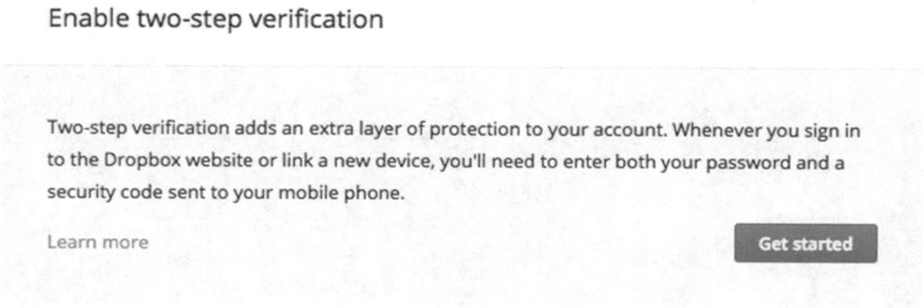

Enable two-step verification

Two-step verification adds an extra layer of protection to your account. Whenever you sign in to the Dropbox website or link a new device, you'll need to enter both your password and a security code sent to your mobile phone.

Learn more   Get started

Figure 2-40. *Screenshot of Dropbox two-factor authentication introduction*

Enable two-step verification

An authenticator app lets you generate security codes on your phone without needing to receive text messages. If you don't already have one, we support any of these apps.

To configure your authenticator app:

- Add a new time-based token.
- Use your app to scan the barcode below, or enter your secret key manually.

Back   Next

Figure 2-41. *Screenshot of Dropbox two-factor authentication introducing generator app*

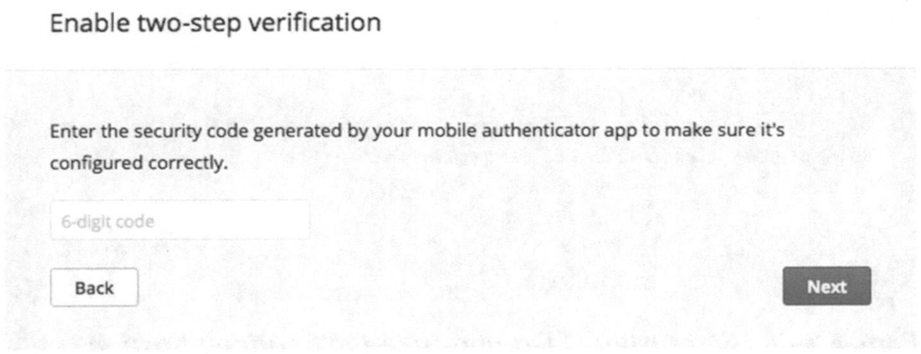

Enable two-step verification

Enter the security code generated by your mobile authenticator app to make sure it's configured correctly.

6-digit code

Back   Next

Figure 2-42. *Screenshot of Dropbox two-factor authentication generated code input*

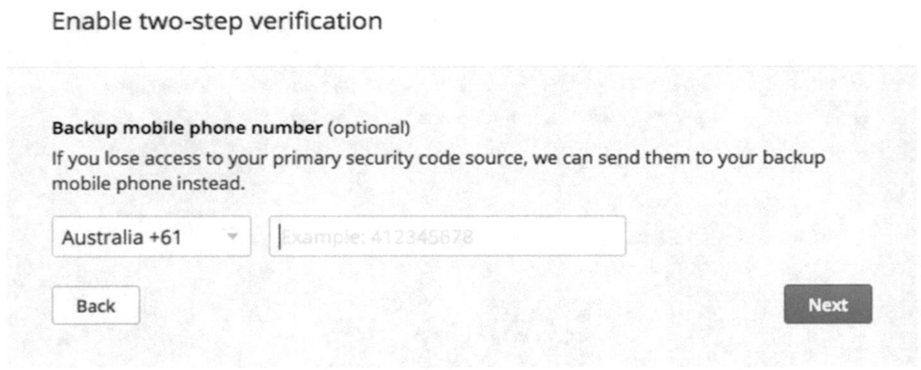

Enable two-step verification

Backup mobile phone number (optional)
If you lose access to your primary security code source, we can send them to your backup mobile phone instead.

Australia +61   ▼   Example: 412345678

Back   Next

Figure 2-43. *Screenshot of Dropbox two-factor authentication phone number input*

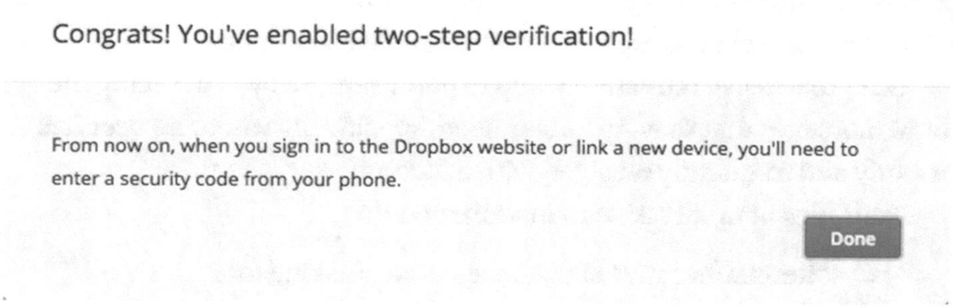

Congrats! You've enabled two-step verification!

From now on, when you sign in to the Dropbox website or link a new device, you'll need to
enter a security code from your phone.

Done

Figure 2-44. *Screenshot of Dropbox two-factor authentication success message*

Pattern: Progressive reduction

Finally, in contrast to progressive disclosure, rather than expanding on information as a user needs it, *progressive reduction* is the practice of reducing detail as a user no longer needs it. Expert users of an interface—loyal, repeat visitors, power users, subject matter experts, specialists—can learn an interface and no longer want the additional help provided to new users. You might reduce coachmarks and help tips after first use or start shrinking and removing labels on buttons. Expert users no longer need training wheels so stop cluttering the interface is with unnecessary information.

To progressively reduce information, remove coachmarks, tutorials, and feature explanations when they are no longer needed and help the expert focus on new content. Restore these extras when the user has not accessed the feature recently. Provide explicit user-initiated links to reduce interface noise, such as "Skip tutorial," "OK, got it," "Not now," "Later | Close," and "Hide this." You might consider pairing progressive reduction with a temporary notification (as described previously) or an inline hint (http://ui-patterns.com/patterns/inline-hints) to indicate where the content may be found in the future, such as a reference guide or user settings. Alternatively, progressively reduce the visibility of features based on recency and frequency of use alone, without intervention from the user. This takes control away from the user, so use with caution.

Use progressive reduction when expert users get tired of seeing the same messages that they no longer need, specifically when the user has recently and frequently engaged with a feature.

Examples of progressive reduction include

- "Remember me" checkboxes to stop asking for usernames and passwords.

- "Don't ask me again" checkboxes to stop asking questions every time a user initiates an action like deleting a file or dismissing a survey.

- Reducing notifications as a user starts ignoring them. Code learning app, Enki, for example, turns off notifications if their daily reminders are ignored for too long.

- Hiding old feed activity. If it's been a long time since a Twitter user has looked at their feed, for example, Twitter will show the last tweet the user saw and fold away all the old activity that has passed since then in favor of showing recent content. The user, however, can tap a link to immediately restore the hidden content.

I think a direct comparison between progressive *disclosure* and *reduction* means that the reduction should directly support the user's level of control—it should be user initiated. Slack, for example, automatically turns off email notifications for new users when they turn on push notifications to the mobile app. Technically this is not user initiated but system initiated. Slack does, however, provide a link to the user's settings, so they may turn the emails back on if they wish. They delicately walk the line of giving the user control as well as making smart guesses at actions to take for the user.

Finally, my favorite example of progressive reduction is apps remembering windows I've collapsed and hidden in the past to let me clear up the interface and focus on my task uninhibited.

Bringing it all together

From here you can begin to recognize patterns across the Internet. Within your own products, you can recognize patterns and where pages differ, which can give you hints about opportunities to consolidate and refine inconsistencies. You've seen how to navigate resources for learning more patterns. Now we'll wrap up how to make the most of pattern resources with an example task of redesigning a login form.

Pattern: Login form

A **login form** (or sign in) asks for an identifier, such as a username or email address, and authentication information, usually a password, to access a user account containing private, personalized information.

Figure 2-45 shows an example of a login form, asking for an email address and password.

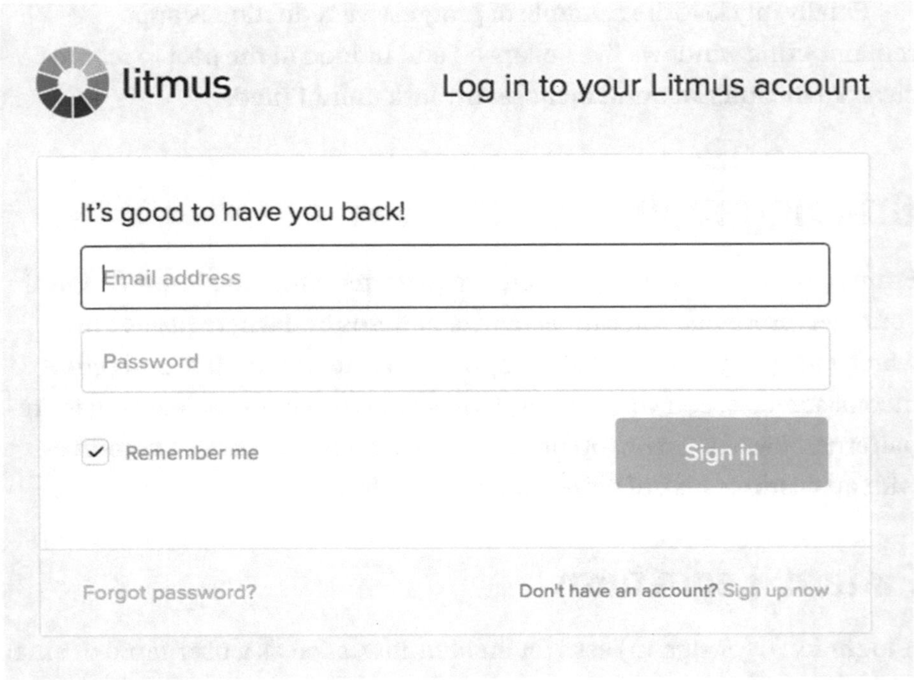

Figure 2-45. *Screenshot of Litmus's login form*

Show a login form to visitors when they need to access their content, either right before performing an action that needs an account (such as following or friending a person) or when directly accessing a "log in" link. When a user submits the login form, you need to check their details, and if they are incorrect, show validation feedback and help them recover—it's common to include a password recovery link in a login form. After successfully logging in, return the user to the content they requested before presenting the login form.

Using an email address as a username is an effective usability hack that's extremely memorable. It also doubles as a unique identifier for the account and a communication channel, so you may contact the user about the account. In this way, a telecommunications company might use a phone number as a username to minimize the number of details the user needs to remember. Alternatively, an identifier could also be a socially recognizable username like a twitter handle, for example, @lara_hogan.

Naturally, you won't need to use a login form if you don't have account registration or if you use the social signup pattern where you'd need to connect to another service instead.

Example: Redesigning a login form

Given the task of redesigning an existing modal, you can explore the modal pattern to inform your design.

Figure 2-46 shows a fictional login form.

Figure 2-46. *You've been tasked with redesigning this login form*

From the pattern

From the details of the login form pattern we've just seen, we can see that we have design decisions to make about when to show the form, how to help people recover from errors, and what to use as an identifier.

Suppose the login form is for an information site that lets you save articles. When you save an article, you need to be logged in so that you can be shown that saved article again in the future. So we'll add some details. Figure 2-47 shows an amendment to include the text, "To save this article, you must sign in to your account."

Figure 2-47. *A reason to log in*

Now you can see why you need to log in to your account and that you can tap a closing "×" to leave.

To help people recover from errors, we'll add a password reset link ("Forgot password?"), as shown in Figure 2-48.

Figure 2-48. *Password recovery*

Finally, for a login identifier, we'll use email address. Figure 2-49 shows "Email address" for the form field label and placeholder text, "e.g. jane. smith@example.com".

Figure 2-49. *Email address as an identifier*

Pattern resources

By researching our pattern resources, we find a few UI frameworks suggest a "Remember me" checkbox to help users stay signed in. Figure 2-50 shows the new checkbox.

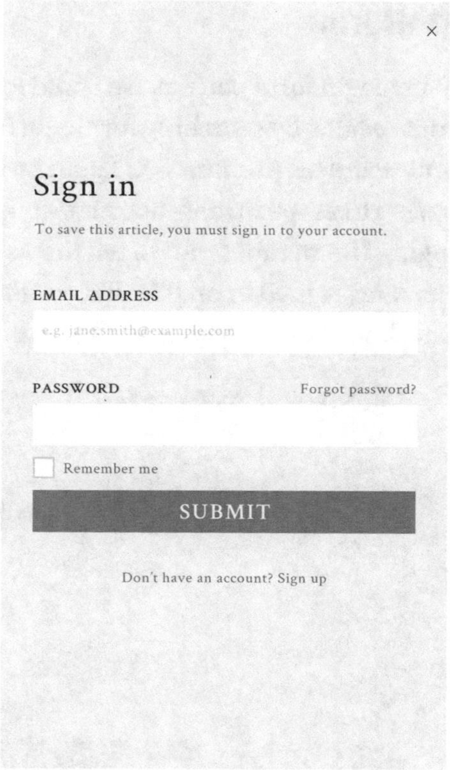

Figure 2-50. *Remember me checkbox*

This approach can help users avoid frequently needing to log in. There's a risk though if your users are accessing your product on shared devices, such as in a university, library, or corporate network: other people may see their content when they leave the device. For this example, we'll assume the majority of users are accessing the product privately on their own personal devices.

Searching for patterns

To learn more about the login form pattern, we could look for "login" or "sign in" to expand our results. By searching for "login form best practices," you can find 3 Rules for Painless Account UX: Login by Jessica Enders (www.sitepoint.com/3-rules-painless-account-ux-login-screens/), which suggests changing "Remember me" to tell the user exactly what will happen. For example, "Stay signed in on this device." Figure 2-51 shows update text for the checkbox label, "Stay signed in on this device."

Figure 2-51. *Stay signed in on this device checkbox*

Our login form is complete.

Competitive analysis

For competitive analysis, we might consider Medium, as it's a high-traffic web site that lets you save articles. Interestingly, Medium shuns the login form pattern in favor of password-free accounts using email (`https://blog.medium.com/signing-in-to-medium-by-email-aacc21134fcd`), as shown in Figure 2-52.

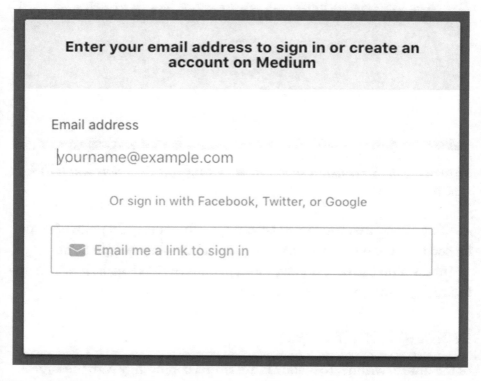

Figure 2-52. *Screenshot of Medium asking only for your email address*

When you need to sign in, Medium will send a magic link to your email address, as shown in Figure 2-53.

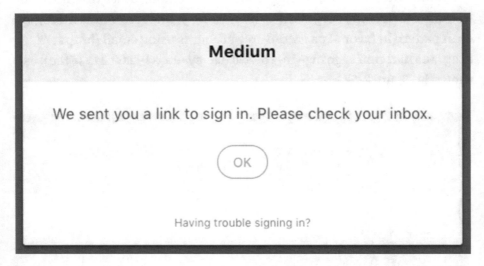

Figure 2-53. *Screenshot of Medium telling you they sent you a link to sign in*

This means that your email account becomes the main point of failure for security. For our example, we'll stick with the simple login form.

Innovation can occasionally make patterns redundant, so maybe in the future login forms won't exist anymore.

Learning from the best

At the time of writing, Facebook is the virtual community with the largest number of user accounts in the world at over 2 billion.[26] To learn from Facebook, we can look at their own login form as well as their login best

---

[26]Wikipedia, "List of virtual communities with more than 1 million users," `https://en.wikipedia.org/wiki/List_of_virtual_communities_with_more_than_1_million_users`.

practices (`https://developers.facebook.com/docs/facebook-login/best-practices`). In their best practices, they suggest you "provide a glimpse of the content available to people prior to logging in." For products with visually compelling content, showing a glimpse of what's to come in a background image could be enticing. For our example of logging in to save an article though, there's not a lot to show. We're done for now.

Summary

We've talked about how to discover new patterns and find examples of them in the wild. We've also learned about these new patterns:

- Walkthrough

- Playthrough

- Newsletter signup

- Validation feedback

- Social signup

- Lazy signup

- Notifications

- Good defaults

- Coachmarks

- Progressive reduction

- Progressive disclosure

- Staged disclosure

Now that you've seen these patterns, be careful to avoid treating them like hammers; not everything is a nail. Next, we'll explore how users find, read, and share content, as a lens for analyzing patterns in depth and deciding which pattern to use and when, so you might see when a pattern *is* the right tool for the job.

CHAPTER 3

Deciding which pattern to use and when

Hitting the right note includes knowing when not to strike.

In this chapter, we'll look at considering the context of your design problem so that you can evaluate a pattern's suitability; not every pattern is appropriate to every problem. For context, we'll consider user needs, technical challenges, and business implications for patterns. We'll explore principles for evaluating the effectiveness of patterns.

Throughout the chapter, we'll see patterns for finding, reading, collecting, and sharing content.

Context

There are a few particular aspects you may consider to define the context of design problems: user journeys, user tasks, personas, constraints, and content or data.

User journeys or customer journeys (https://conversionxl.com/customer-journey-maps/) are the story of how a user navigates your product, including how they perceive your product at every touch point on their way toward their goal. They describe the setting and sequence of events. Journeys encompass discovery and awareness of your brand,

© Diana MacDonald 2019
D. MacDonald, *Practical UI Patterns for Design Systems*,
https://doi.org/10.1007/978-1-4842-4938-3_3

first use of your product, conversation across channels including social media, loyal engagement, and actions taken with your product.

User tasks or Jobs to be Done (`https://blog.intercom.com/finding-jobs-your-product-is-used-for/`) establish what your user is trying to accomplish, such as find a restaurant's opening hours, play to kill time waiting for a train, update social status, or crop unwanted details out of a photo.

User groups or personas (`www.nngroup.com/articles/persona/`) can be used to describe the identities and experiences of your users. A person's interaction with your product is influenced deeply by their personality, motivations, expertise, location, mood, etc., and that's not even touching on their demographics.

Constraints include all the limitations set on a solution. This ranges from the user's environment including their devices (phone, TV, watch), Internet connection (fast, patchy, filtered), and input mechanism (track pad, keyboard, voice, touch screen) to your technology, business, and design needs. There might be ethical, legal, resource, or security constraints that influence your design choices.

Content and **data** include all the substance of your product. Content usually means copy (text), images, video, and all other media and information, including user-generated content like photos on social media. Data often describes information about the user or product like search results, current address, or filenames.

In the following text, we'll see how each of these factors influences when a pattern is appropriate.

Pattern: Autocomplete

The **autocomplete** pattern automatically completes typed user input with matching results from a larger data set.

As human beings, as flawed, mere mortals, your site visitors cannot always recall the full name of what they're searching for, or how it is spelled, or even what you happen to call it. As such, autocomplete lets your system match your visitor's first few key strokes with possible solutions. Autocomplete will usually attempt to finish the word you have started, like in predictive text on mobile phones, saving you keystrokes and time, while efficiently finishing the task. This is extremely convenient when accurately typing a phrase is difficult, such as on mobile phones, graphic tablets, voice control, and so on.

Figure 3-1 shows the SwiftKey keyboard, which will let you autocomplete the previously typed text "de" with "design," "dev," or "development" in a single tap.

Figure 3-1. *Screenshot of the SwiftKey keyboard*

In search, autocomplete is often used to promote popular results, such as Apple matching "iph" to "iPhone" and specific results like "iPhone XR" and "iPhone 8 and iPhone 8 Plus," as shown in Figure 3-2.

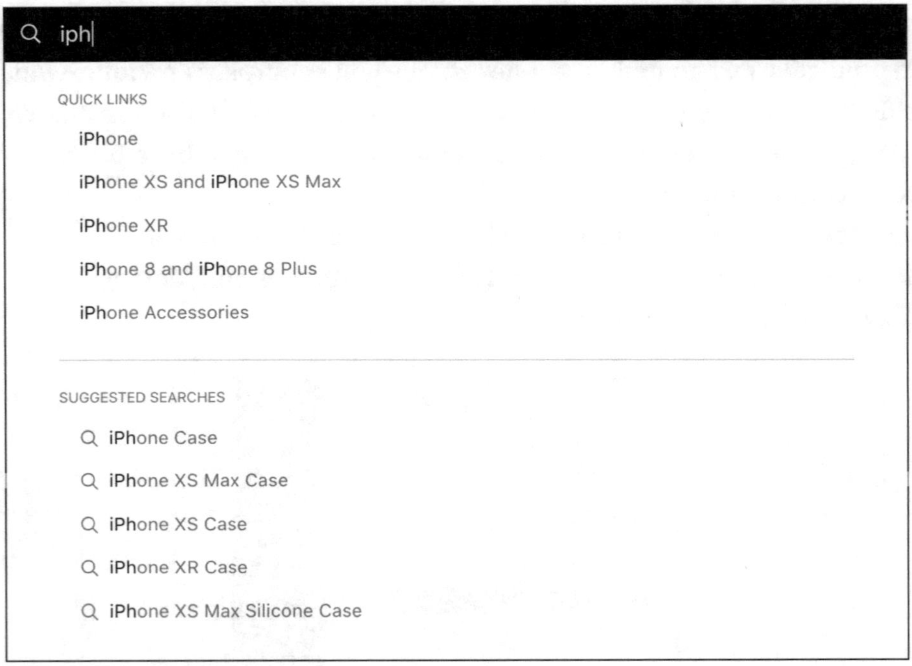

Figure 3-2. *Screenshot of Apple's autocomplete search that suggests quick links to specific products and suggested searches to related products like cases*

Autosuggest

Similar to traditional "autocomplete," "autosuggest" breaks beyond the input provided to suggest alternative, relevant answers. It might even suggest results from multiple data sets. For example, after the United Kingdom voted to leave the EU, it's been suggested that afterward many people in that country began searching Google for "What is the EU?"

and "What is brexit?"[1] As you can see in Figure 3-3, Google lets you autocomplete the words "what is the europea" with "what is the european union," showing the text that you can autocomplete by pressing the Tab key ("n union") in light gray text in the search input field.

Figure 3-3. *Screenshot of Google's autocomplete highlights the differences in text that you can complete*

Google also blends autocomplete and autosuggest by letting you autocomplete the whole sentence using other noun phrases, showing additional results below the search input field (emphasizing the available autocomplete text with strong, bold text).

In Figure 3-4, you can see Google also autosuggests similar phrases, such as "what is europe saying about brexit," that can be quite different from the text you've typed so far, "What is Brexit EU?".

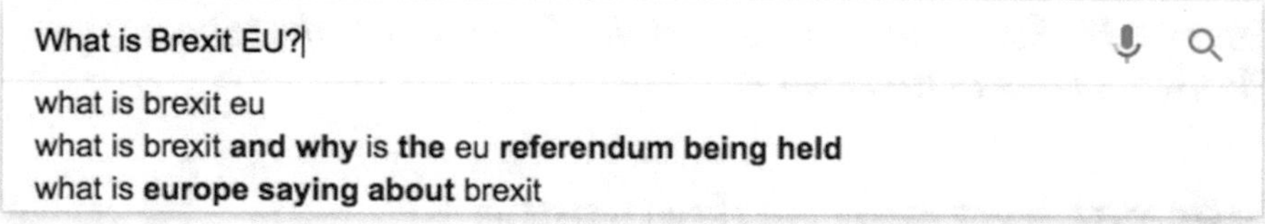

Figure 3-4. *Screenshot of Google's autosuggest that proposes alternative queries that might be relevant*

---

[1]Alina Selyukh, "After Brexit Vote, Britain Asks Google: 'What Is The EU?'," www. npr.org/sections/alltechconsidered/2016/06/24/480949383/britains-google-searches-for-what-is-the-eu-spike-after-brexit-vote, June 2016.

Another occasion to use autocomplete is when you might use a different name for the same idea, like showing "autosuggest" in results for "autocomplete."

Immediately showing results the moment a user asks for them is necessary to provide feedback about how the system behaves. Without snappy feedback, the user might see no results at all and be unable to access what they need. If you've typed an entire phrase before the autocomplete presents results, you might miss the functionality completely. If you searched for "iPhone 77" without seeing any autocomplete results, you'd miss the result linking directly to the "iPhone 7" product, see regular search results, as shown in Figure 3-5, and never know the autocomplete existed.

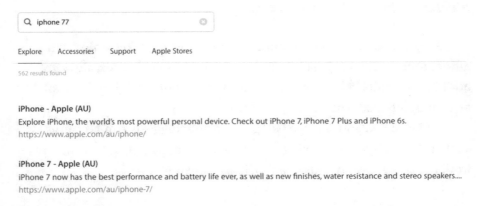

Figure 3-5. *Screenshot of a search for "iPhone 77" that shows the iPhone 7 as one of two results*

User context and performance

There are any number of reasons your autocomplete might be too slow. Both the processing needed to find matches and the rendering of results take time. If there's any search-side processing performed (for large data sets), your user's patchy Internet connection on the train home might be a problem. If there are complex results to show like product images, your user's old mobile device with a poor CPU and dying battery might have insufficient power to render results quickly. Figure 3-6 shows images in autocomplete search results that might have performance considerations.

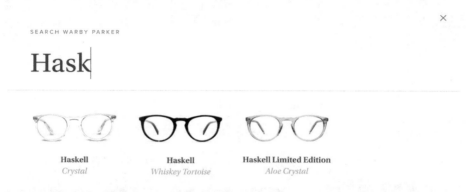

Figure 3-6. *Screenshot of Warby Parker's site presenting product photos with their names in autocomplete search results*

In these contexts, autocomplete is probably a poor solution. To otherwise help users navigate a large set of results, you might instead use pagination and search filters, which we'll look at shortly. To be forgiving of a user's misspellings, you might use spell check or present alternative (correctly spelled) results after they've finished typing.

To learn more about autocomplete pattern design, see Baymard Institute's 8 Design Patterns for Autocomplete Suggestions (`https://baymard.com/blog/autocomplete-design`).

Pattern: Search filters

Search filters reduce search results by excluding irrelevant information using contextual filters to refine initial results.

Figure 3-7 shows an example of search filters.

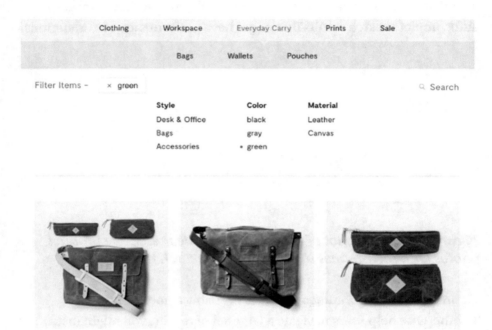

Figure 3-7. *Screenshot of Ugmonk searches, which can be filtered by style, color, and material*

Search results can be massive. The typical Google search produces millions of results, and most of the results will not be seen. To find a needle in a haystack like that, a searcher *might* try a different search term with fewer results, or you could provide search filters through which your user can indicate which aspect of the results they are most interested in.

Search filters are great when the searcher doesn't know exactly what they're looking for but have some criteria in mind by which they'll recognize the right result when they see it. For example, your user knows they want to see a new movie and they don't know which movie yet, but they do know what genres they like, directors or actors they admire, which cinemas nearby they'd like to see a movie at, and what time of day they can see a movie. In this scenario, your user can make their preferences known by using your filters to narrow the full list of currently showing movies down to those that fit their needs.

Using search filters, your users can dynamically update results with contextual options that they may not have even considered before to narrow down the search. See, for example, Birdsnest's (www.birdsnest. com.au/womens/dresses) rarer filtering options, such as "body shape," shown in Figure 3-8.

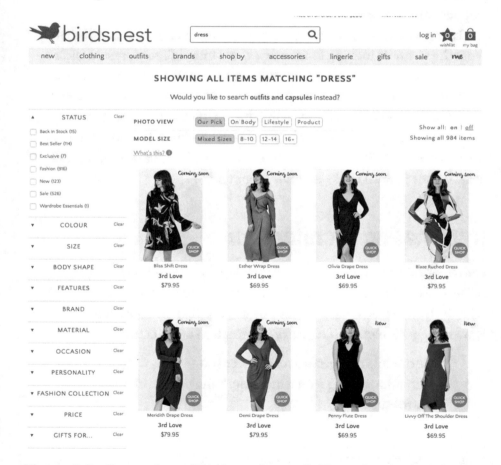

Figure 3-8. *Screenshot of Birdsnest's search filters that include body shape, occasion, and personality*

Use the search filter pattern when traits are obvious like media type (maps, images, books), price, and size. Avoid this pattern when categorization is hard, when there are very few results, or when clear navigation and hierarchy is more suitable.

Search filter patterns are often seen with scoped search, where you first choose some larger exclusive category, like dresses or jeans, before showing search filters relevant to their results, like maxi dresses or straight cut jeans. We'll look more at mixing and matching patterns and their implications in Chapter 6.

Using a filter is basically a crutch for being unable to instantly divine what the visitor is looking for. Ideally, you'd immediately present their exact desires. You might find alternatives to search filters for discerning their needs, such as seeing they've come to your site from an ad for blue hats, and instead of showing a search listing filtered to "hats" that are "blue," show only a result listing containing blue hats. No clutter, no distractions. This illustrates how the user journey and task could prove the search filter pattern irrelevant in this context.

Information architecture

Information architecture is the structure of your product's information—how it's organized and labeled. Organizing your product effectively helps users find content by its grouping and relationships. Dan Brown suggests eight principles of information architecture:[2]

1. Principle of *objects*: Treat content as a living, breathing thing with a lifecycle, behaviors, and attributes.

---

[2]Dan Brown, "Eight Principles of Information Architecture," www.designprinciplesftw.com/collections/eight-principles-of-information-architecture.

2. Principle of *choices*: Create pages that offer meaningful choices to users, keeping the range of choices available focused on a particular task.

3. Principle of *disclosure*: Show only enough information to help people understand what kinds of information they'll find as they dig deeper.

4. Principle of *exemplars*: Describe the contents of categories by showing examples of the contents.

5. Principle of *front doors*: Assume at least half of the web site's visitors will come through some page other than the homepage.

6. Principle of *multiple classification*: Offer users several different classification schemes to browse the site's content.

7. Principle of *focused navigation*: The principle of focused navigation–don't mix apples and oranges in your navigation scheme.

8. Principle of *growth*: Assume the content you have today is a small fraction of the content you will have tomorrow.

These are solid foundations for evaluating patterns. The search filter pattern itself embodies the principles of *choices* and *multiple classification*. In applying the pattern, consider how the search filter labels might *exemplify* the items within each filter. Filter by "category" or "type" gives you no indication of whether these filters will help a user in their search. Alternatively, filter by "weather" or "color" gives them a sense of what they might find underneath. By considering the principle of *growth*, you might conclude that while your horizontal filter toolbar design[3] looks fine now with just four filters, as the number of results grows, you might not fit the extra filters needed to sufficiently winnow the results. Conversely, as the collection grows, you might need to be more judicious in only showing the most valuable filters, occasionally culling some.

This brings us back to considering the context of your data and the user's journey. For example, Airbnb shared in a video about search at Airbnb[4] that filtering by price and deal-breakers were in the top four most important aspects to their users' searches, and so they prioritized the price filter as well as easy access to the many deal-breaker filters (like pet-friendliness) in their design.

Multiple filters

Sometimes search filters let you select multiple filters at the same time. To clarify how two filters work together, you can show the matching criteria in the results. For example, using Birdsnest's search filters, you can select items that are less than $30 or more than $150. In the results you can then see the prices and which products match each of these criteria, as shown in Figure 3-9.

---

[3]Christian Holst, Baymard Institute, " Filtering UI: A Horizontal Toolbar Can Outperform the Traditional Sidebar," https://baymard.com/blog/horizontal-filtering-sorting-design, May, 2015.

[4]Airbnb on YouTube, "Search @ Airbnb," https://youtu.be/l2ywLWyRjA8?t=312.

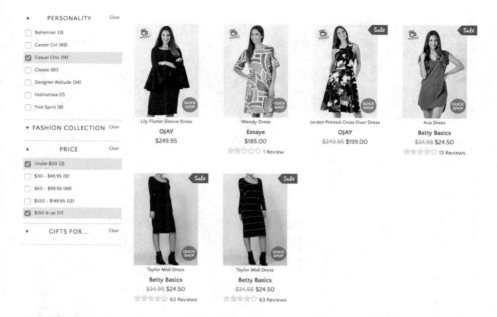

Figure 3-9. *Screenshot of Birdsnest's search filters, which let you choose several filters*

It might seem obvious for "price" that a dress is only one price, so selecting two price ranges (less than $30 and more than $150) should find products priced in both ranges rather than no results, but it's less obvious if choosing "Casual chic" and "Classic" will find products in both those styles or only products that are classic *and* casual chic. Feedback is needed to clarify filter functionality.

Filter feedback

To give users more feedback when they interact with your filters, you can subtly reinforce filter behavior, without cluttering results by using matching images. Here you can see in Figure 3-10 product images with the models' arms shown when you filter by the "Show Off Arms" body shape.

Figure 3-10. *Screenshot of Birdsnest where product images match filters*

There's no need to add text to each result to say "shows off arms" when it can be seen from the photos. In contrast, the price needs to be shown as text next to each item.

Another method to give feedback about search filters is using tags to show the selected filters, as you can see in Figure 3-11. This is particularly helpful on smaller screens where you may be unable to show filters and results at the same time and therefore unable to indicate which filters are selected in the filters themselves. If the tags were not shown here, you would be unable to see that the results are filtered at all.

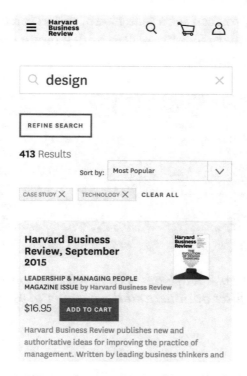

Figure 3-11. *Screenshot of Harvard Business Review, which shows the refined search results are case studies about the technology industry*

Choosing filters

The filters offered must meaningfully classify and describe the results. To illustrate, a filter for "good movies" will be challenging because the criteria for deciding what's good are highly subjective, so it will be unclear what results are in each filter. If, however, you clarified the filter as "BAFTA award-winning films," some clear criteria for "good" are being used, and the results will be more predictable.

In Figure 3-12, you can see a search term and a search filter for "what" kind of job, a filter for "where," as well as further options to refine the search, including salary bands.

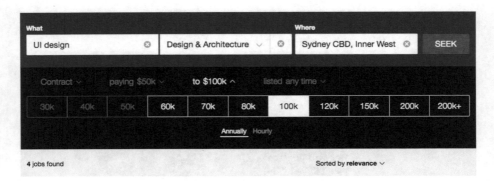

Figure 3-12. *Screenshot of Seek's filters, which show available filter options, selected filter options, and the number of results*

Live filters

Refining results in real time using "live" filters—instantly updating results—lets your users directly manipulate the results and gives them control to respond to feedback: each set of new results lets them know whether they need to add another filter to find content right for them. For example, if your user's first refinement still shows millions of results, they know they need to keep filtering. During the process of updating the results, you can convey what's happening to your users by presenting a loading state and then a completed state. The loading state might animate the old results out and new results in to draw attention to their changes. The completed state might cease all movement or add a visible detail to the filter after results are loaded, which indicates it's "on." For tiny screens, you might be unable to fit the results next to the filters, requiring a different approach to how you present the loading state. Instead, you might batch filters.

Batch filters

You might let your users batch together their filter choices by selecting a few filters at once and choosing "Search," "Apply," or "Done" before presenting any results. This is particularly useful if your product has a lot of data. Otherwise, your user might be frustrated by irrelevant, distracting information until they've added the final filter necessary to produce the results they want. Google Analytics updated their UI in early 2016 to let users navigate different reports, select "data granularity," and add additional dimensions *before* updating the results. Previously, any selection would immediately block all subsequent interaction until the results had updated (a time-consuming activity) before you could select anything else needed to actually filter the data to the results you wanted. Figure 3-13 shows Airbnb's batch filters.

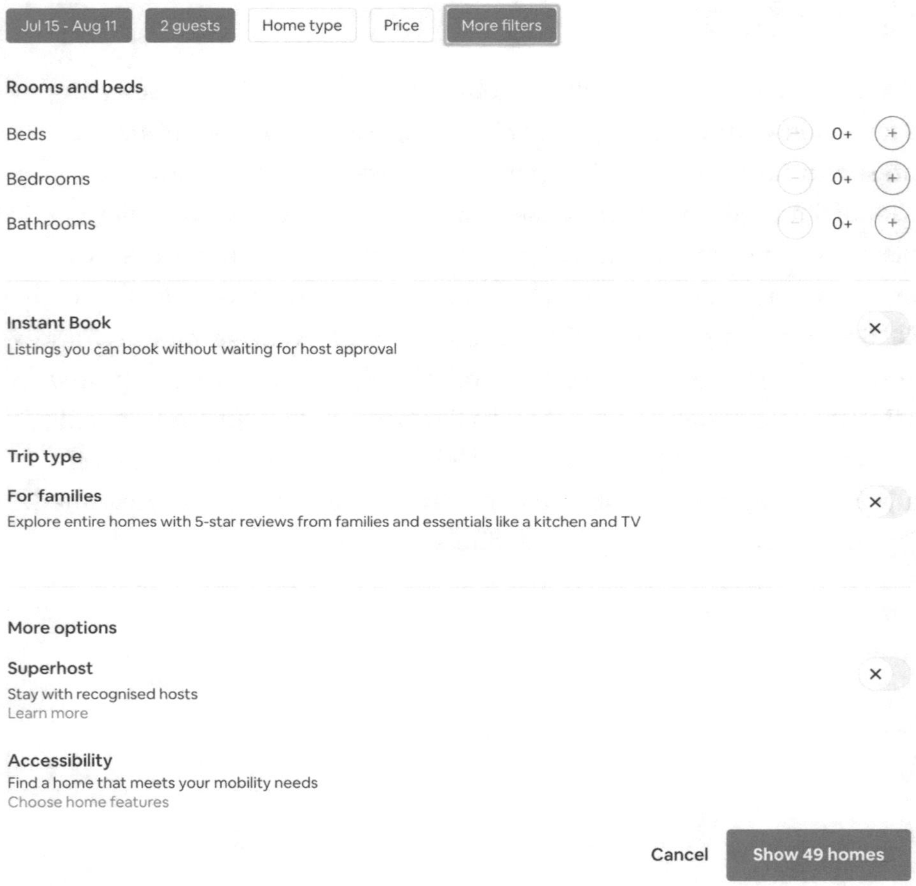

Figure 3-13. *Screenshot of Airbnb's batch filters*

These filters let you select the number of rooms and beds, toggle "superhosts," choose amenities, and tap "See homes" before processing results.

Error prevention and recovery

Nobody likes zero results, so nudge the user toward successful searches. This will depend a lot on the shape of the data. Show the most important filter first. Show how many results will be available with subsequent filters, or prevent access to additional conflicting filters. Avoid filters that only match single items. Figure 3-14 shows Airbnb's price filter.

Figure 3-14. *Screenshot of Airbnb's price filter*

This filter shows results at each price point using a miniature bar chart and a range slider, indicating areas that would produce zero results.

Using a "clear filters" option provides people with an emergency exit when the results are bad so they can abandon their choices so far and start over.

Pattern: Activity feed

An **activity feed** shows recent activity in a timeline—a list of events in chronological order. Activity feeds help users keep up to date on changing events and information that are important to them. They're common staples of social media sites.

Figure 3-15 shows an example of an activity feed.

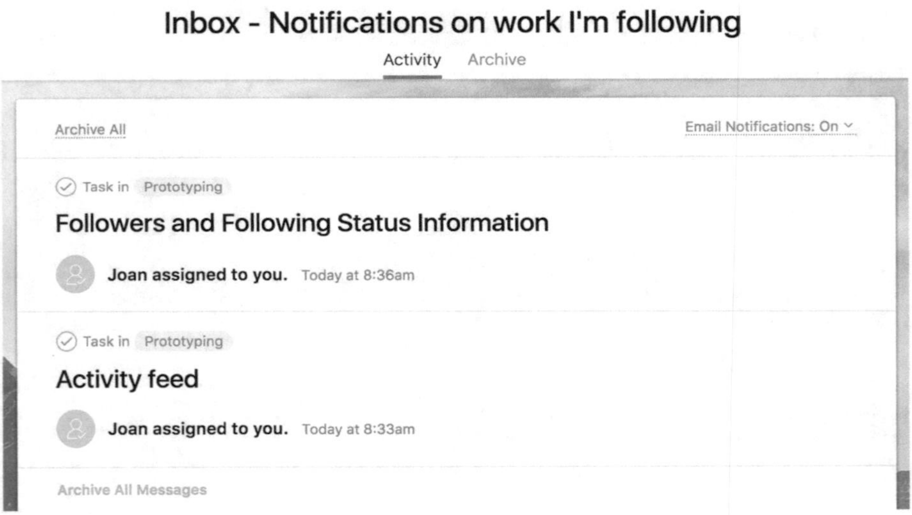

Figure 3-15. *Screenshot of Asana's activity feed, which shows tasks assigned to you by other members, the projects they belong to, and by whom*

It can be difficult sometimes to keep up with everything that's happening. Within a product, there might be a whole community and ecosystem of activity and countless events occurring at any moment. By using an activity feed, you can help people identify events that matter to them in a sea of noise, and then engage further with that event and your product. This is particularly helpful when a lot can happen between the times a user engages with your product, such as reading the world news in the morning and catching up on the last day's events.

As activity feeds are used to enable users to look through information, scannability is a high priority. You can segment activity into digestible little chunks, where the visitor may then leap off into further related action on an activity, if they wish. Alternatively, they might continue on consuming the stream without acting on events.

To aid scanability, think about

- Showing when an event occurred (more on that in the following text).

- Exactly what happened—What's the nature of the event? A photo uploaded? A status update? Money sent? An item shared? A new task to do?

- Clearly indicating who initiated an event, such as prominently showing a user's display photo and name or handle in a social media activity feed.

    - If there are multiple parties involved, visually demonstrate the relationships between them, such as listing an individual user as well as the organization they belong to.

To show events over time, it's important to make the time the event occurred visible, relevant, and useful. Your product will determine what's "relevant," but here are some examples.

- For a blog or news site, show the day, month, and year. Is the exact time a post was published useful to your users?

- In a real-time social media feed like Twitter, where drama can unfold quickly, show the date and time down to the minute and maybe even seconds.

- For a health and fitness app, show today's events or this week's progress. While the year's summary might be useful, it's unlikely each event like a workout or meal eaten is interesting in a timeline of that period.

Instead of absolute dates and times like "1 January, 3:24PM," it's sometimes more pertinent to show relative times like "3 minutes ago" or time between milestones, such as "While you were away" or "Yesterday." The older content is, the more likely it should be archived in away in a larger category like "Older than 5 years ago."

Once a user finds something of particular interest in an activity feed, you might let them take further action, like

- Follow a link to read more. For example, follow a news teaser to the full article.

- Save the event. For example, bookmark a shared social object.

- Manipulate or interact with the event. For example, comment on an event, complete a task, remove from the feed.

Given the repetition of these available actions for a large number of items in a feed, you might hide the actions a user can take until they interact with the event, such as showing "share buttons" and other controls on hover for nontouch devices or after tapping to select the event on touch devices.

To help users track recent events that matter to them, an activity feed needs to effectively manage the volume of activities. Too little activity might mean your product isn't providing enough value and appears quiet or boring. Too much activity and the user might be overwhelmed, defeating the purpose of the feed. For high volumes of activities, some clustering may be needed. For example, you might collapse all of "Sam's" recent activity—sharing hundreds of photos—into a single "Sam" photo album event.

Further, you might offer separate views of the same feed, such as Facebook providing a main feed as well as notifications for a particular activity you're interested in, such as activity by certain people.

Note   Facebook kicked up a stink when they stopped showing content chronologically and started presenting information according to its perceived importance. This had the unfortunate side effect that conversations became difficult to follow when comments weren't presented in order. Usually, activity feeds are shown in order according to time the event occurred. Conversely, Reddit masterfully elevates highly voted content in its comment activity feeds, making an effort to clearly show the filtering that's happening and maintaining coherence.

An activity feed may be a poor choice when your most interesting content is not the most recent.

Pattern: Favorites

A list of **favorites** is a personalized, curated list of preferred items, stored for later use.

Figure 3-16 shows an example of favorites, labeled as "Likes."

Figure 3-16. *Screenshot of Twitter's likes, which create a shorter feed of happy content*

Favorites serve two primary functions. Firstly, users can return to content they adored in the past. Secondly, users can find favorited content recommended by others; favorites reveal exceptional and remarkable content in a saturated environment.

Note   In rare cases, favorites are private. This is akin to e-commerce "wish listing" when a user is shortlisting candidates or saving a product for later, such as when they've saved up enough money.

A rose by any other name

The favorite pattern can go by many different names, while the behavior underpinning stays the same. Pinterest, for example, lets you "save" a pin to mark it as a favorite. Twitter, by contrast, lists a user's favorite tweets under "liked" tweets. Notably, both of these products have changed their naming conventions and features over the years to pare back and simplify their UIs. Pinterest experimented with both a "like" and a "save" button before retiring like as a redundant option next to the more powerful "save" that let users categorize their favorites. Twitter renamed their previously existing "favorites" as "likes," which suits its more generic behavior. A liked tweet could have all sorts of social implications, according to personal use and behavior in particular circles. Some people treat it only as a reaction and never refer back to their likes.

To use the favorite pattern, you'll need to let people mark an item as a favorite as well as refer back to the collection of favorites. You can let people add an item to their favorites by providing a button on or next to the critical items in your product, such as articles, photos, or activity. You can let your user—and in some cases, other users—refer back to the collection of favorites by keeping them all in one place and linking to each individual favorited item.

While it's common to store all of a user's favorites in a single list, if your users want to show *why* they added an item to their favorites, you could let them group and name their favorites in several named lists like Pinterest's "boards," as shown in Figure 3-17.

Figure 3-17. *Screenshot of a product design board on Pinterest with 21 saved pins*

On the other hand, housing favorites together in one list with a single name makes them more a versatile feature: a favorite could be a read receipt to acknowledge you've seen it, it could be a bookmark of bad content you want to fix later, it could literally be your single most loved item.

Favorites are often accompanied by a metaphor and iconography such as heart, star, thumbs up, or "+1" to like, love, promote, or collect an item. For usability, ensure consistency and standards are used instead of switching between a heart here and a star there. Likewise, showing both the icon and label in all the places a favorite appears can avoid the confusion of an unlabeled heart shown in one place and an ambiguous label like "saved" with no matching icon elsewhere. If for some reason you use both a thumbs up for favorites and a "+1" for up-voting content (e.g., in a democratic system promoting crowdsourced ratings), make it clear what the distinction is between them.

It's worth considering how the favorite pattern is different from similar features.

Favorites tend to reflect particular affection toward an item and are usually shared, making it a social experience, distinguishing favorites from traditional browser "bookmark" or "save for later" features, which are personal and unremarkable. Further, bookmarks usually grab a whole page instead of one specific object within the page.

Favorites are also *collected* unlike reactions, such as a "like" on Facebook or "comments," which are more ephemeral and transactional in nature, often forgotten, and rarely referred back to. In the case of Twitter, a user's "likes" list is prominently displayed on their profile.

A favorited item also offers only a single indicator of a user's general preference for it rather than showing on a scale just how much it matters to them. By contrast, "ratings" let a user specifically rate an item using, for example, an overall number out of 5 or on particular attributes like Airbnb's "cleanliness" and "value" ratings.

Favorites and activity feeds are shaped around bite-sized, shareable content. As such, it's easy for search engines to identify highly influential content produced from within these patterns. Here you can see how some patterns naturally support search engine optimization (SEO).

Microcopy

Throughout all of these patterns, you'll find most have important interface text guiding the user. **Microcopy** alludes to the smaller snippets of text in an interface used to guide and reassure a user, as opposed to long-form copy like a blog post. Some common microcopy examples include

- Link text, button text, headings, and navigation labels that help people find their way about, usually front-loaded with important, skimmable keywords

- Validation feedback, inline help text, tags, labels, and tooltips, oriented around user tasks, suggesting specific solutions or next steps

Microcopy is necessary for people to navigate and complete tasks, as well as being useful in inspiring trust and credibility. Clear microcopy may also reduce customer support queries by addressing people's concerns before they ask. As proof of the potential impact of these tiny words, read about The $300 Million Button by Jared M. Spool (`https://articles.uie.com/three_hund_million_button/`), wherein 35 words increased the number of customers purchasing by 45%, by replacing the "Register" button with a "Continue" button and the message: "You do not need to create an account to make purchases on our site. Simply click Continue to proceed to checkout. To make your future purchases even faster, you can create an account during checkout."

As with validation feedback (described in Chapter 2), good microcopy is concrete, precise, active, and positive and suggests solutions. It is also more important than ever to cull needless words.

Pattern: Pagination

Pagination separates large bodies of content into separate pages, accessed by a shared index of links.

Figure 3-18 shows an example of pagination.

Figure 3-18. *Screenshot of WordPress pagination, which shows the number of items, the current page, the total number of pages, and navigation buttons*

When navigating large data sets, it can be overwhelming to view a large quantity of data at once. Pagination can be used to reduce the results down to easy-to-digest chunks. In some cases, this has the added benefit of improving page performance and preventing data download issues. Each page shows some set number of results like 10 search results or 20 products.

Pagination is often combined with tools to customize display options like sorting, choosing number of results per page, and adapting content. We'll look more at mixing and matching patterns and the resulting confusion in Chapter 6.

Where to draw the line

Pagination needs to adapt to the size of the results to effectively chunk content. For 1–5 pages, you might show a direct link to each page: 1, 2, 3, 4, 5. For 100 pages, you might collapse the index down to Start, Previous, Current, Next, End, or 1, 2, [...] 99, 100. For 1–5 results (larger items like products in a range), you might opt for "Previous: <Product name>" and "Next: <Product name>" (similarly for relevant articles: "Next: 10 things you didn't know you were doing wrong with pagination"). For this latter example, you might also let touch devices swipe between paged results.

Finally, you might consider a canonical "view all" page[5] for medium data sets where you *can* display all items at once without melting your visitor's device, but you *start* by showing a limited set. These little labels drastically change the clarity of the pattern.

Pagination is sometimes forced upon users to increase ad views per article, rather than user-centered reasons. To make sure pagination adds value to the experience, consider paginating where a user might want to bookmark or share a specific, digestible subsection in a longer piece. One benefit to pagination is its accessibility.

Accessibility

Accessible digital content has these traits:

- *Perceivable* (people can become aware of it)

- *Operable* (people can use it)

- *Understandable* (it naturally makes sense)

- *Robust* (can withstand evolving technology and still be perceivable, operable, and understandable)

If you're using semantic elements like links to navigate to different pages within your paginated content, you don't need to do much extra to make it perceivable and operable.

Sometimes UI patterns are implemented with components using Accessible Rich Internet Applications (ARIA) attributes[6] that give more information to Assistive Technologies to increase accessibility.

Let's explore a related pattern with different accessibility challenges.

---

[5]Google Webmaster Central Blog, "View-all in search results," https:// webmasters.googleblog.com/2011/09/view-all-in-search-results.html, September 2011.

[6]Mozilla Developer Network, "ARIA," https://developer.mozilla.org/en-US/ docs/Web/Accessibility/ARIA.

Pattern: Infinite scroll

Infinite scroll, sometimes more accurately called "continuous scroll," loads and presents more results as you scroll without interruption in a single stream (seemingly forever, hence the moniker "infinite scroll").

The content is loaded exactly in proportion to the user's scroll effort, disclosing only as much information as they're interested in and giving a hint of what's to come, as we saw in the progressive disclosure pattern in Chapter 2. We can reduce clutter and minimize cognitive load on users with a minimal interface and give them *control* to expand it as they choose.

By presenting the most relevant content first, the user may then continue for as long as they are interested. As they approach the end of the currently displayed content, you can start to load more in the background. To avoid a user ever having to wait for content (knowingly, impatiently), you can pull in more items each time you load a set and start loading before they've reached the bottom, while they're still reading other items. This means never seeing the dreaded "loading spinner." If your user does reach the bottom before you've pulled in new content, you can show a stylized placeholder dummy image (a "loading skeleton") to set expectations about what's happening (loading) and what will happen (an item of about this size and shape will load). An example of this is shown in Figure 3-19.

Figure 3-19. *Screenshot of Facebook's placeholder story hints at content to come*

Infinite scroll is ideal when your visitor wants to keep consuming your content for extended periods, with limited deviations or engagement. Use this pattern when the user wants ever more content, such as social news feeds (e.g., Facebook, Twitter) and photostreams (e.g., Instagram, Google image searches). Unlike search results, you are not filtering for an exact place to stop, you are only looking for "more."

Check out Etsy's case study where continuous scroll ruined their user engagement (http://danwin.com/2013/01/infinite-scroll-fail-etsy/) because no one would leave their infinite scroll to commit to a particular product to buy for Fear Of Missing Out (FOMO) on better things yet to be seen.

There are limited use cases where infinite scroll is appropriate, such as photostreams. Avoid infinite scroll when you want to bookmark, save, or share specific content in the stream. If you want to support that in an infinite scroll, you might take extra care to offer a "save for later" feature or a link that will take you directly to that item. Avoid it when you need to stop and engage with results like favoriting (see the favorites section ahead). Avoid infinite scroll when visitors need to compare items or find specific items. Avoid when visitors need to see your site footer.

As you can see, the task the user wants to accomplish shapes how appropriate infinite scroll is in a design problem's context. Further, infinite scroll is notoriously challenging to implement well technically,[7] so your technical resources and time may make this a poor choice. The success of infinite scroll is also heavily influenced by the context of what content and data you have. If there's only one additional set of results to load, there's little value to using the pattern.

Principle of choices in action

One design consideration for infinite scroll is how to offer a reader choices in navigating the content; they might want to skip a section of content and jump to another section further along. Twitter will hide old Tweets if you've been away awhile, so you can then choose either to skip to new Tweets or tap to expand more Tweets, seeing older, previously collapsed Tweets. If your user wants to jump to a specific section in your content like "results starting with U," pagination indexed by letters might be more effective. See pagination earlier.

Note that as infinite scroll keeps loading more content, it can be difficult to reach the footer of a site (it will be pushed out of sight just as you arrive). You might handle this by removing the site footer on pages that use infinite scroll or offering adjacent links to skip to footer and stop loading content.

---

[7]Surma and Robert Flack, "Complexities of an Infinite Scroller," https://developers.google.com/web/updates/2016/07/infinite-scroller.

Principle of disclosure in action

A variation on infinite scroll is lazy-loading content on demand. That is, instead of scrolling to indicate your user wants more content, they can tap a button like "Show more results" to start loading more. Your user has a taste of what's to come before choosing to disclose more.

Figure 3-20 shows an example of the principle of disclosure in action in an infinite scrolling blog.

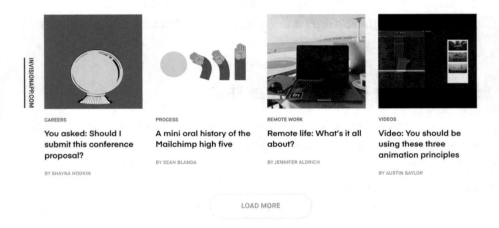

Figure 3-20. *Screenshot of InVision's load more button, which leaves space for more content to load inline*

This distinction is important: it's almost a pagination "Next" button that lets people access the site footer but sacrifices the ease and non-committal nature of scrolling. Imagine choosing to open another bag of cookies (a conscious decision) vs. continuously snacking from a very large bowl that's constantly being topped up. There's a decision point.

Inclusive design

One tactic for ensuring an accessible interface is to practice inclusive design. Inclusive design practices can ensure a functional, usable, and desirable experience for more people. Infinite scroll can impact accessibility,[8] making it hard to design an infinite scroll that supports a wide variety of users and input mechanisms like keyboards.[9] To design an inclusive infinite scroll, you can

- Announce changes in the main content area where new content is loaded to screen readers using ARIA live regions (`https://developer.mozilla.org/en-US/docs/Web/Accessibility/ARIA/ARIA_Live_Regions`).

- If you use a loading spinner or skeleton, ensure its content is perceivable by diverse users. You might, for example, announce the loading information to screen readers using the same `aria-live` method.

- Manage content focus for users with keyboards or screen readers. If you offer an explicit button to load more content in your pagination component, you'll need to move the user's focus to the new content. You might use JavaScript to `focus` the first element of the newly loaded content and apply an attribute— `tabindex="-1"`—to the element if it's not normally interactive, such as a static text heading.

---

[8]Level Access, "Infinite Scrolling – Impact on Accessibility Series: #1 Common Issues," `www.levelaccess.com/infinite-scrolling-impact-on-assistive-technologies-series-1/`.

[9]Ana Crespo, "Infinite scrolling is probably not a good idea for your website," `www.nomensa.com/blog/2015/infinite-scrolling-probably-not-good-idea-your-website`, May 2015.

To learn about implementing design patterns accessibly, check out The A11Y Project (`http://a11yproject.com/`). For an in depth reference, I refer you to Heydon Pickering's book, *Inclusive Design Patterns*.

Infinite scroll vs. pagination

Infinite scroll and pagination patterns both segment large collections of content. In both cases, users want to browse some smaller proportion of the total content available. In contrast, using neither of these patterns would mean loading huge amounts of content on one page (imagine Pinterest loading all its billions of images at once). Infinite scroll might make it *feel* like all the content is there, even though you know it's loaded a chunk at a time, while pagination makes it clear you're viewing just one segment at a time. The context for your design problem will suggest when each solution is a fine or frightful fit. If your user is a teenager casually indulging in photos to pass the time, infinite scroll is likely better. If your user is a nurse scavenging for an answer to a question, pagination may be the superior choice. In assessing these patterns for your case, explore how the user groups and personas, tasks, and constraints build the context.

Infinite scroll and favorites

As we saw in the section on favorites, it's useful to refer back to favorited items. Twitter's web site (at time of writing) offers no native ways to search your Twitter favorites and lists liked tweets on an infinite scrolling page. If you want to refer back to an older favorited item, you need to keep rapidly scrolling, nudging the bottom of the page, and waiting for more tweets to load until you find the one you were looking for.

Figure 3-21 shows a loading spinner at the bottom of Twitter's infinite scrolling "likes" feed.

Figure 3-21. *Screenshot of the bottom of Twitter's infinite scrolling "likes" feed*

To avoid this clunky search behavior, you might use pagination instead or consider pairing your infinite scroll with search and filters. We'll talk more about this in Chapter 6, on mixing and matching patterns.

Pattern: Follow

The **follow** pattern lets people subscribe to receive a stream of frequently updating content of interest to them, either around a certain topic or from an individual or organization.

Figure 3-22 shows an example of the follow pattern on Medium.

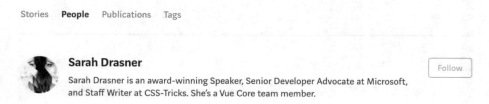

Figure 3-22. *Screenshot of Follow Sarah Drasner on Medium*

The primary objective is to let people curate their information consumption, only hearing highly tailored, relevant news.

This lets followers consume content at their leisure, like trawling through a Twitter feed on the bus. Following also indicates which content a follower is interested in, so they might only receive updates about a specific person, organization, or topic. A fan might find following your Facebook page easier than checking your blog every day to see what's new.

In order to make use of this pattern, your users need to follow enough topics or people to see as much content as they desire. To help users find people to follow, you can make recommendations based on previous activity, other similar users, or similar topics and people. Pinterest asks users up front what topics they're interested in during the signup playthrough, shown in Figure 3-23.

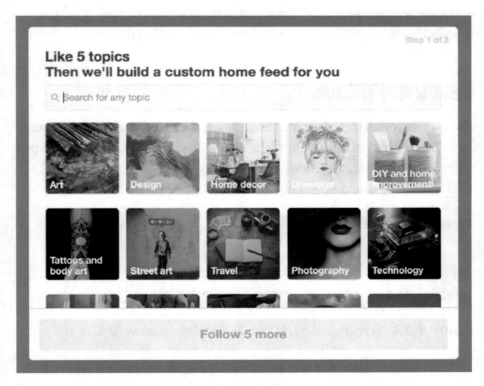

Figure 3-23. *Screenshot of Pinterest asks you about five topics to customize your home feed*

As you can see, followed entities can be used to populate activity feeds.

Use the follow pattern to increase engagement when you have evolving on-site content where a particular author or topic may be of interest while vast swathes of other content are not interesting to the follower.

Unlike the friend's list pattern (ahead), there is no expectation that a followed party will follow someone back.

Pattern: Friend's list

Similar to the follow pattern, the **friend's list** pattern lets users signup to receive updates about other people's content, as well as connect directly. Both parties must agree to be friends to share content. This helps people connect through their mutual interests.

Figure 3-24 shows an example of the friend's list pattern.

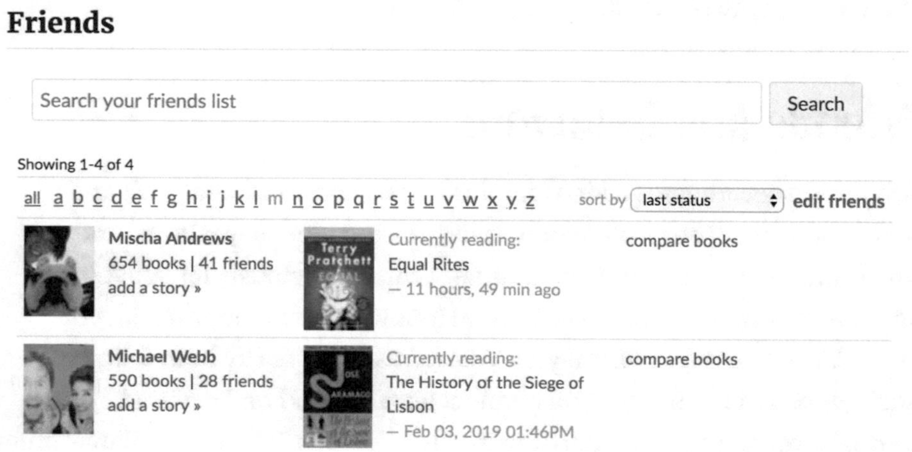

Figure 3-24. *Screenshot of Goodreads friendships, which tell you what your friends are currently reading*

It is necessary for each friend to confirm the relationship; therefore, it must be possible for users to find each other (potentially by searching for an address, name, username, or other identifier) and for one party to initiate the connection (usually by "adding a friend"). After connecting, the friend's list pattern provides greater access to each friend to communicate and share content.

Use this pattern when social interaction between users is critical to the product. If connection between users is incidental to the product, then it might be better to support connections on another platform, such as helping users find each other via following your product on LinkedIn, rather than creating a redundant friend ecosystem.

The context for assessing the suitability of the friend's list pattern includes consideration for where each party is in the user journey. Social networks often make friend suggestions for you to connect with people when they receive signals that you might have already met, such as sharing mutual acquaintances, attending similar events, and so on.

Friends and followers

As you can see, there is a lot of similarity between the friend's list and follow patterns. They may also co-exist in a blended way within the one product or platform. For example, Twitter previously let you follow someone with no expectation of them following back, but then let you share direct messages only if you "friend" each other (by both following each other). In contrast, if you connect with a friend on Facebook, you mutually recognize the friendship, but it's also possible to "unfollow" them to stop seeing their posts but stay friends, letting you both send direct messages and still access posts via your profiles.

We'll look more at mixing and matching patterns in Chapter 6.

Interaction and motion design

Beyond the foundations of exploring patterns by context, it's useful to consider the interactivity of patterns. Human–computer interaction has a long history. Fitts's Law—which states the time to reach a target area is related to the distance and size of the target—has been around since the 1950s. In interaction design, it's used to optimize interfaces by minimizing travel between targets or activities and increasing the size of targets, such as the clickable area of a link, so that users may perform tasks efficiently.

For some rules of thumb about usability, check out Jakob Nielsen's 10 Usability Heuristics for User Interface Design (`www.nngroup.com/articles/ten-usability-heuristics/`). Likewise, for interaction design heuristics, see First Principles of Interaction Design by Bruce "Tog" Tognazzini (`https://asktog.com/atc/principles-of-interaction-design/`).

Animation on the Web, or motion design as it's increasingly called, is only now growing into a mature field. Importantly, it can be used to orient and direct attention, improving user satisfaction through superior feedback and by expressing tone, as discussed in Navigating the World of UX Motion Design.

Note   For an approachable and comprehensive lesson in motion design, Val Head's book *Designing Interface Animation* shares concrete examples of purposeful design, driven by user needs, built using modern performance and progressive techniques.

For use in evaluating patterns, let's look at the triggers, action, and feedback of interaction.

Triggers

Every interaction must be initiated by some trigger, such as a button. That is, a trigger uses a visual or social signifier that some action will take place and, when triggered, will start the process.

Effective triggers are recognizable with a clear relationship between what they look like and what they do. For example, when using the favorite pattern, the trigger to favorite an item might be a heart button with the word favorite placed closely together with the item. A high-five emoji with no text might be less clear as a trigger to favoriting some content.

Some interactions have no visible signifiers to signify their existence. For example, when you pinch to zoom in on an image, there's usually no visible evidence that this interaction is possible. Mostly these triggers are taught socially, and expectations are set through convention (picture galleries on phones can frequently be navigated by swiping). And yet you can hint at available behaviors using subtle signifiers, such as overlaying images with a magnifying glass to suggest zooming is possible.

Figure 3-25 shows when tapping Vermont's map of Gant stores using one finger, they use an overlay to tell you to use two fingers to move the map.

Figure 3-25. *Screenshot of Vermont Gant's store locator showing "Use two fingers to move the map" on touch*

This lets you both scroll the page—without being "caught" in a map—and pan the map with a different gesture if you want to traverse it.

Triggers can be reinforced with positive results to associate the trigger with good things and, in turn, encourage more interaction with the trigger. With this in mind, consider spending more time on designing triggers that are used with high frequency to ensure they're satisfying and delightful. Twitter, for example, fill their gray heart icons with red on hover and animate their hearts with sparkles (`https://css-tricks.com/recreating-the-twitter-heart-animation/`) when tapped so that the trigger itself is considered enjoyable.

Action

The action itself should be close to effortless. There's no need for a drag and drop interface if there's only ever one drop target area—a click/tap will do there.

Minimize the amount of coordinated movement needed; "scrubbing" back and forth through a video or audio player or using a slider should let you clumsily drag the marker about rather than require precision to reach the desired place. For this interaction, you might

- Use well-spaced "steps" to ensure a price slider lands easily on $100 instead of $98.2

- Provide keyboard shortcuts

- Include "skip forward"/"skip backward" buttons with defined increments

- Control scrubbing speed with upward/downward touch or mouse movement

Feedback

For feedback, keep the results of an action as close to the trigger as possible to keep the user's attention and give them a sense of direct control or manipulation over the object they are interacting with. If the results need to be some distance away, as in the case of search filters, for example, you can use timing and animation to reinforce the relationship. You might provide additional contextual feedback, such as validation feedback or a notification (see Chapter 2).

This feedback is an opportunity to thank and reward the user for their effort. As with the Twitter heart animation example, you can jazz up the trigger itself or you can introduce the results with personality using delightful microcopy or animations that float, jiggle, or fade.

When is a pattern a bad idea?

Patterns are the natural result of successful, proven methods for solving user interface problems. In turn, a pattern is a poor choice when you're faced with a totally novel problem that's yet to be solved. While you might lean on the principles we've discussed in this chapter to evaluate a new user flow or interface solution, it's a bad idea to shoehorn old solutions into new problems. We take a deeper look at breaking away from patterns in Chapter 6.

I'd also suggest not trying to use a pattern when you haven't yet defined the problem! It might be tempting to reach for the comfort of a pattern when faced with the uncertainty of an ill-defined problem. Hold off until you can clearly articulate who your audience is, what their motivations are, and what they're trying to achieve with your product.

Finally, patterns are useful as named solutions to clarify and communicate about user interfaces. If you find yourself splitting hairs trying to distinguish between very similar patterns, they're no longer communicating the way patterns are supposed to.

Example: Login form

To expand on our example from Chapter 1, let's see how we can use what we've learned in this chapter to make some changes.

Firstly, our user journey shows that our user has just arrived at the login form from reading an article. Using more precise microcopy, we'll tailor the form to include a link back to the article. Figure 3-26 shows the added text "back to article."

BACK TO ARTICLE ×

Sign in

♡ To save this article, you must sign in to your account.

EMAIL ADDRESS

e.g. jane.smith@example.com

PASSWORD   Forgot password?

☐ Stay signed in on this device

SIGN IN

Don't have an account? Sign up

Figure 3-26. *The precise label used is "back to article"*

By using a text link to return to the article, we now have a descriptive label for the cross icon. Instead of adding an `aria-label for "back to article"` on a `cross icon`, we can use an `aria-hidden` attribute so the cross isn't misread to screen readers. If we didn't use aria-hidden, the full link might read as "back to article times operator." Note that we've also updated the button's call to action to match the title and avoided the jargon of "submit," which can sound mechanical.

Using the information architecture principle of front doors—at least half of your visitors will come through a backdoor (or some page other than the homepage)—we can check that our login form makes sense when you've arrived from different places. When you've come from an article, you'll see three clues to give you a sense of where you are and what to do next: "Sign in," "Back to article," and "To save this article, you must sign in to your account." If you had clicked directly a "log in" link, we could hide the back link and help text, and the form would still make sense.

For users accessing this form on their mobile devices, it could be difficult to write out their full email address. We could use the HTML input type=email attribute to ensure the "@" symbol is shown on mobile keyboards. Figure 3-27 shows the changed keyboard.

Figure 3-27. *Example of the email keyboard on iOS devices include an easy-to-access at symbol (@) and a full stop (.)*

The user task underpinning our example login is that the user wishes to save their article. If we are using the favorite pattern, we *could* be more explicit about what impact the action of logging in will have. Figure 3-28 shows more text to explain: "To add this article to your public list of favorites, you must sign in to your account."

Figure 3-28. *Example of login form with more explicit impact described*

It's a little wordy though. To balance the usability of a minimal aesthetic, we might simplify it a bit, as shown in Figure 3-29: "To like this article, you must sign in to your account."

Figure 3-29. *Example of login form with balanced microcopy and minimal aesthetic*

Finally, in considering motion design and feedback in interactions, if a user submits the login form with an empty email address, we might jiggle the email input field to draw the user's attention to it.

We've used our analysis of patterns to make a few tiny improvements. Achieving many tiny improvements can lead to big results.

Summary

Now you know how to discover new patterns as well as how to analyze them. To kick off your analysis, you've seen how to clarify your design problem's context in terms of journeys, tasks, personas, and constraints. We've also covered these patterns:

- Autocomplete

- Search filters

- Infinite scroll

- Pagination

- Activity feed

- Favorites

- Follow

- Friend's list

Next, we'll dive into internal pattern libraries where patterns are tailored to the context of your organization.

CHAPTER 4

Patterns in design systems

There is a saying that every nice piece of work needs the right person in the right place at the right time.

—Benoit Mandelbrot

In this chapter, we'll clarify some terms around patterns and design systems, look at growing a design system, and along the way we'll discuss some decisions you might need to make.

What's in a name? The devil is in the details

A word of warning: language is a fickle thing and some people will attribute different meaning to one word, some people will use different words to describe one idea, and the meaning of all those words will evolve. This is particularly relevant in a young industry like digital design with rapidly changing technology and norms. We haven't yet settled on a consistent understanding of patterns and design systems as an industry. Given that, I'll do my best to paint a picture for you and discuss these ideas in terms of how you can use them, regardless of what you call them.

© Diana MacDonald 2019
D. MacDonald, *Practical UI Patterns for Design Systems*,
https://doi.org/10.1007/978-1-4842-4938-3_4

Pattern libraries

A **pattern library** is a collection of patterns, used to *communicate* and *improve design decisions*. This includes reusable solutions to problems focused around interaction and UX components. In a broad sense, a pattern library is a collection of abstract UI patterns, such as you would find in the pattern collections I mentioned in Chapter 2's resources, including UI-patterns.com and UIPatterns.io. In these, you'll find a single pattern might be illustrated with dozens of varied examples of its use in the wild.

Popularly though, you'll find the term "pattern library" used to describe an internal library within a single organization, which is often more specific—tailored to the one entity's needs. Here, you would find each pattern has only one main visual representation as it is applied to the organization (where it has a visual representation at all).

Note   In instances where you find more than one visual representation of a pattern in a library, you'll usually find that the style is the same, and only subtle variations are shown. For example, there might be light and dark themes of the pattern to be used in different parts of the product.

Design systems

A **design system** is a single source of truth for shared parts and processes, such as components, patterns, and guidelines, to build consistent products. It's the ecosystem in which the design process occurs and the output of design thinking reaches its intended audience. The term can encompass all of the design, code, and content resources we'll discuss shortly. Design systems are tailored to organizational needs.

Additionally, design systems reflect the culture, team values, and visual language of an organization. Likewise, they address matters of "scaling" design quality. That is, design systems ensure high standards of design quality are maintained in a large and growing organization instead of falling into chaotic, splintered customizations. In large systems, they may inform design with user research.

That said, sometimes people use the term "design system" to refer to narrower definitions of design guidelines or visual language, which we'll examine next.

Related design, code, and content resources

As a digital practitioner, you might be familiar with other design and code resources in the world related to patterns: style guides, style manuals, brand manuals, identity guidelines, front-end style guides, templates, and so on. In many cases, they're complementary ideas that work well together. In other cases, you'll find these housed together under one name (whether a "pattern library," a "design system," or something else). In order to know when and how to use each of these resources, you'll need to understand the finer differences between them.

Let's explore what you might use or encounter out in the world.

Editorial style guides

Style guides, **style manuals**, or **tone of voice guidelines** focus on the written word to set standards about communication styles to ensure consistency in tone, choice of words, punctuation, grammar, and other language decisions. You may recognize the more famous standards set by Chicago Manual of Style or The Oxford Style Manual. To differentiate style guides from other resources, you might consider them "editorial style guides." Sometimes, style guides may also include material around content, such as imagery and laying it out.

Figure 4-1 shows an example of an editorial style guide.

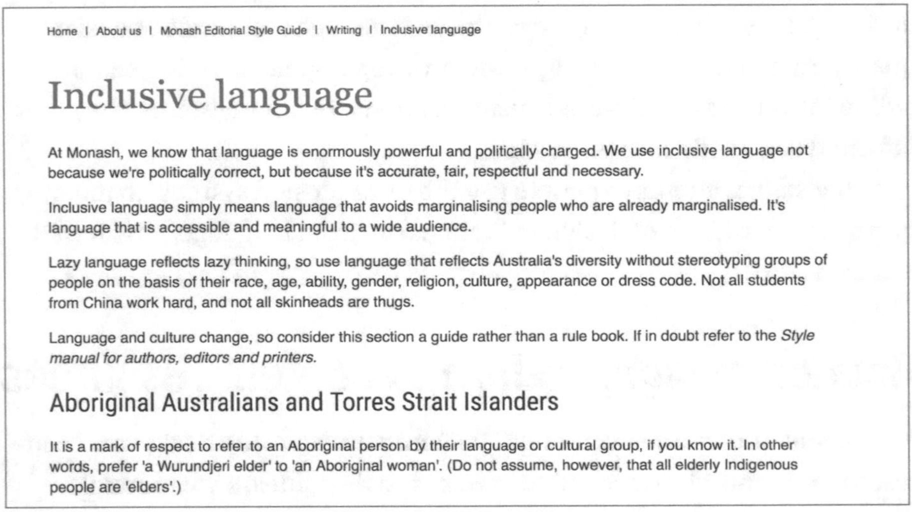

Home | About us | Monash Editorial Style Guide | Writing | Inclusive language

Inclusive language

At Monash, we know that language is enormously powerful and politically charged. We use inclusive language not because we're politically correct, but because it's accurate, fair, respectful and necessary.

Inclusive language simply means language that avoids marginalising people who are already marginalised. It's language that is accessible and meaningful to a wide audience.

Lazy language reflects lazy thinking, so use language that reflects Australia's diversity without stereotyping groups of people on the basis of their race, age, ability, gender, religion, culture, appearance or dress code. Not all students from China work hard, and not all skinheads are thugs.

Language and culture change, so consider this section a guide rather than a rule book. If in doubt refer to the *Style manual for authors, editors and printers*.

Aboriginal Australians and Torres Strait Islanders

It is a mark of respect to refer to an Aboriginal person by their language or cultural group, if you know it. In other words, prefer 'a Wurundjeri elder' to 'an Aboriginal woman'. (Do not assume, however, that all elderly Indigenous people are 'elders'.)

Figure 4-1. *Screenshot of Monash University's editorial style guide*

If your organization has a lot of text-heavy user-generated content, you may need publicly accessible editorial style guide content. Wikipedia, for example, is written collaboratively by more than 69,000 active contributors, providing a Manual of Style[1] and a Simplified Manual of Style[2] to help "editors write articles with consistent and precise language, layout, and formatting, making Wikipedia easier and more intuitive for users."

Meanwhile, if your organization has a lot of text-heavy content created by many internal employees and contractors, such as a knowledge base or help documentation, you may need to provide a privately accessible resource covering how to communicate with your customers or audience.

---

[1]Wikipedia, "Manual of Style," https://en.wikipedia.org/wiki/
Wikipedia:Manual_of_Style.

[2]Wikipedia, "Simplified Manual of Style," https://en.wikipedia.org/wiki/
Wikipedia:Simplified_Manual_of_Style.

These considerations may dictate whether or not your editorial style content is part of your design system. Atlassian's design system (`https://atlassian.design/`) takes the rare approach of including both public and restricted content including their public Voice and Tone guide,[3] linking to their public Language & grammar page[4] and their restricted page for "Writing error messages."

Brand guides

Brand guides, **brand kits**, or **visual style guides** lean toward visual matters of a brand's identity, including logos and icons, color palettes, typography, and photography. They are sometimes mixed in with editorial style guides. One key difference between editorial and brand/visual style guides is that branding guidelines can be used by external parties, such as Instagram's brand guidelines (`https://en.instagram-brand.com/`) that suggest how you may use their logo, when to request permission, and respecting their trademarks. Figure 4-2 shows one guideline from Instagram's brand guidelines to "Balance the Instagram Brand with your brand."

---

[3]Atlassian, "Voice and Tone," `https://atlassian.design/guidelines/voiceAndTone/personas`.

[4]Atlassian, "Language & grammar," `https://atlassian.design/guidelines/voiceAndTone/language-grammar`.

01

Balance the Instagram Brand with your brand

Avoid representing the Instagram brand in a way that:

• Makes the Instagram brand the most distinctive or prominent feature.

• Implies partnership, sponsorship or endorsement.

• Puts the brand in a negative context as part of a script or storyline. You must comply with our **Terms of Use** and **Community Guidelines**.

Figure 4-2. *Screenshot of one of Instagram's brand guidelines*

For a business such as Instagram's, it's likely that people will want to show off their presence on Instagram in highly visible broadcast media such as film and television. They have a great incentive to help people use their brand assets correctly as well as respect their brand and its contributing members.

For brand material in your design system, consider including

• Downloadable assets such as logo files in vector formats and high-resolution bitmap formats

• Specifications for colors and typography

- Usage and attribution guidelines for names, taglines, photography, and icons

- How to make requests for permission to use any element of a brand or access to assets

These might also be linked from a "media" or "press" page on your site.

Note   For more examples of brand assets and guides, check out Find Guidelines (`http://findguidelin.es/`).

Design guidelines and visual language

Design guidelines describing **visual language** as distinct from brand or visual style guides usually address conceptual topics. Material Design, for example, defines a consistent metaphor to use throughout designs in the Material Design style.

Material is the metaphor

Material Design is inspired by the physical world and its textures, including how they reflect light and cast shadows. Material surfaces reimagine the mediums of paper and ink.

—Material Design's Principles (`https://material.io/ design/introduction/#principles`)

Figure 4-3 shows Material Design's design guide to the visual language.

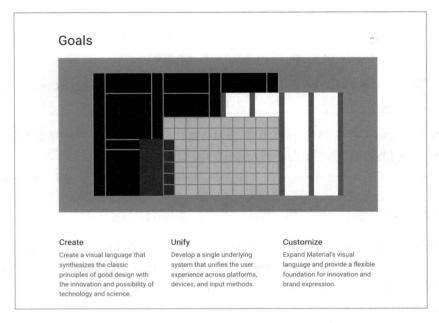

Figure 4-3. *Screenshot of the goals of Material Design*

Note   To learn more about the material metaphor, watch Google's design video about Making Material Design (`https://design.google.com/videos/making-material-design/`).

Dan Mall asserts in Researching Design Systems (`http://v3.danielmall.com/articles/researching-design-systems/`) that design systems should have guidelines for perspective, point of view, and extending creative direction. What's different about your organization? "Otherwise, we all might as well use Material Design and call it a day."

On a similar note, Matthew Ström wrote What makes a good design principle? (`https://matthewstrom.com/writing/principles.html`) about thinking about design principles at *The Wall Street Journal*.

He describes a shortcut that is one of my favorites for using with teams: format design principles as "Even Over" statements, such as "Accessibility even over aesthetics." This is a great method for establishing meaningfully polarizing design principles that sets your organization apart from others as well as highlighting differences in what each designer in your organization values.

Style guides relating to code

Each of the following are extremely similar and tightly coupled forms of design resources touching code, but each is worth mentioning and some distinction can be useful.

Front-end style guides

Front-end style guides are kind of like patterns in action for an organization, shipped with code snippets, design assets, and anything else necessary to actually complete day-to-day design and development tasks affecting the front-end of product.

Figure 4-4 shows Salesforce's Lightning Design System (`www.lightningdesignsystem.com/guidelines/overview/`), initiated by Jina Anne.

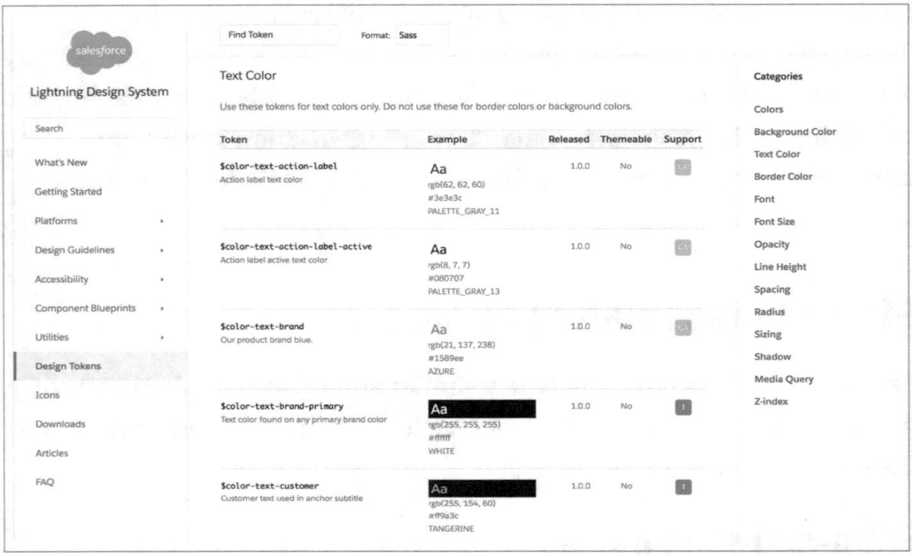

Figure 4-4. *Screenshot of Lightning Design System Design Tokens*

The design tokens for "Text Color" in the Lightning Design System include several examples of describing and showing colors, useful to day-to-day decision-making for designers and developers.

In her book, *Front-End Style Guides* (`www.maban.co.uk/projects/front-end-style-guides/`), Anna Debenham describes a front-end style guide's purpose: "to make building and maintaining a website easier." Her book has a strong focus on development tools and processes to maintain a web site that adheres to intended styles. In her view, a front-end style guide is written in the same markup and uses the same CSS that is used on the "real" web site, and "grows organically with a site throughout its lifetime, acting as a reference and preventing duplication of code and design patterns." These are useful distinctions from other resources and suggest a consideration for any design system: does the design system site need to be built using the same foundations as the product?

> **Note**   The pioneers of UX, Nielsen Norman Group, propose 25 common UI components you'll likely find in a front-end style guide (`www.nngroup.com/articles/front-end-style-guides/`).

Living style guides

Living style guides refer to guides that are in sync with the production environment; change an element in a living style guide and it will change in production across your entire web site (or other digital products). They're designed to give you space to share your design thinking about elements like typography decisions, but also keep guidelines in line with its actual execution. This avoids teams updating branding guidelines but having the development re-brand work to meet the new guideline falling behind.

In many living style guides, the style guide is built straight from the style source code.[5] This can mean that the style guidelines are led by developers. In some cases, that may be prohibitive to designers and other parties wishing to contribute that are not working in the code base. That friction has potential to limit the growth of an organization's design maturity.[6] In other cases, however, that approach may be fine because design is "well integrated in the product development process," indicating reasonable design maturity. Potentially, some designers and contributors may be comfortable working with markup and styles in code, so this approach could even help with collaboration in some organizations. This is a useful consideration for establishing processes in a design system.

---

[5]For advice on this, see Ben Robertson's "Build a Style Guide Straight from Sass" (`https://css-tricks.com/build-style-guide-straight-sass/`).

[6]To learn more, see Stephanie Gonzalez's "Design Maturity: Yesterday vs. today" (`https://medium.com/@InVisionApp/design-maturity-yesterday-vs-today-654f6495c5b2`).

> **Note**   You may use UI development environments, such as Storybook (`https://storybook.js.org/`), to build components separately from production code bases so that front-end development can move ahead of back-end development. Combined with a living style guide as in React styleguidist (`https://react-styleguidist.js.org/`), this becomes a powerful workflow.

Code style guides

Code style guides or **code standards** often focus on the code formatting and naming conventions of a software engineering team, such as whether they use tabs or spaces to indent code and how they name methods. One example is the formalized standard "PSR-2" for PHP.[7]

Code style guides are often quite divorced from design matters. As such, they're often stored separately from design-oriented style guides and design system resources, housed in a code base README page or a code repository's wiki. Typically, only developers have access to these.

There might, however, be some crossover. For example, imagine if the brand guide proposes a color of #fe6481 that is referred to as the brand's "primary brand color," and yet the code style guide specifies a named Sass variable, $brink-pink: #fe6481; as per Name that Color.[8] This discrepancy may lead to mis-communications when designers and developers are talking to each other about colors.

---

[7]PHP Framework Interoperability Group, "PSR-2 for PHP," `www.php-fig.org/psr/psr-2/`.

[8]Chirag Mehta, "Name that Color," `http://chir.ag/projects/name-that-color/#FE6481`.

Google Style Guides,[9] for example, specify their conventions for writing code. Their HTML and CSS guide[10] specifies that CSS class names should not be "presentational" like `.button-green`, but they can be specific like `.video`. Meanwhile, Google's Material Design design guidelines include presentational components like "cards" and "dividers." This difference in attitude might not cause any issues if they're used in different environments by different people, though there's a chance they could cause conflict. One area it could produce an issue is when striving for matching names between design components and code components to improve communication and being limited by conflicting guidance on naming conventions.

You might consider sharing access to these resources, linking them to each other, or potentially storing them together in the one design system.

Component libraries

Component libraries, **UI libraries**, or **code libraries** provide front-end code for UI components (a.k.a. widgets, modules, chunks, blocks). Internally, you might use a component library as a shared collection of UI snippets implementing patterns that anyone in the organization can contribute to building. Check out the U.S. Web Design System's open-source UI component library (`https://designsystem.digital.gov/components/`). Unlike UI frameworks such as Bootstrap, component libraries are tailored to specific purposes, like an internal brand.

---

[9]Google, "Google Style Guides," `https://github.com/google/styleguide`.

[10]Google, "Google HTML/CSS Style Guide," `https://google.github.io/styleguide/htmlcssguide.html`.

An internal component library comes with many of the same challenges that open-source projects do, including matters of versioning and deployment. They also come with product marketing and management challenges, such as roadmap planning, release planning, adoption challenges, and product announcement communication challenges.[11]

Note   There is an interesting relationship between component libraries and developing design patterns. Pure UI (`https://rauchg.com/2015/pure-ui`) lets you edit the width and height of a tooltip on the page and watch the tooltip adapt to the new sizes in real time, as illustrated in Figure 4-5.

---

[11]To learn more about design systems with component libraries as products, I suggest reading The Design System Product by Charlotte Jackson (`https://medium.com/ansarada-thinking/a-design-system-product-cebb3a0b3f1e`) and Nathan Curtis's series on Releasing Design Systems (`https://medium.com/eightshapes-llc/releasing-design-systems-57fca91a23f6`).

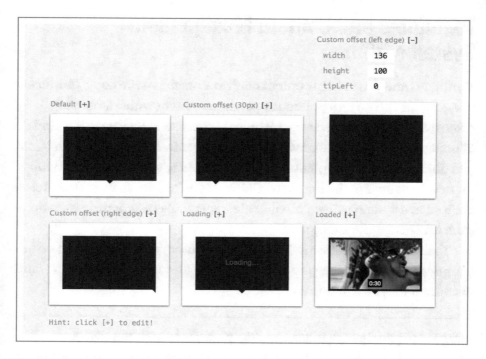

Figure 4-5. *Screenshot of Pure UI with live editable components*

By putting real data (such as desired width and height values) in a component library preview, you might start to see the limitations of a component for the problem you're trying to solve. For example, if you want to display a lot of copy and imagery inside the tooltip pictured, that could suggest that you don't really want a tooltip—which typically contains optional, supplementary information—and what you really want is a thumbnail. If the available components don't support the behavior you need, you might be prompted to consider the patterns behind them and what different patterns and new components would fulfill your need.

Templates and Content Management Systems (CMSs)

Templates and CMSs help content contributors that write copy, produce imagery, and so on independently produce content without needing extensive design knowledge or technical expertise. A **template** is a kind of boilerplate, a bunch of preset layouts, elements, configurations that let you duplicate an existing solution and swap out specific copy and media for new instances of the template. **CMSs** let you create, view, edit, or delete content in a system using a predictable, repeatable system process, where each article can use a template.

To use templates effectively, your contributors might use guidance in your design system to suggest which patterns they need to use for the kind of content they're working with.

Note   Products like Asana provide customers with templates (https://asana.com/templates) within their sites and products as "good defaults" (like we saw in Chapter 2) to help them get the most out of the product without learning good patterns of behavior and interaction from scratch by trial and error. Instead, these customers can lean on the expertise of Asana and others that have worked with countless organizations to discover best practices.

Building design systems using patterns

So we have a better idea now of the finer differences between different design, code, and content resources and how they're used. Given that, what might motivate you to build a design system? How could you use a design system and what would you need to include?

Design systems aim to help teams *communicate* and *improve design processes*. Specifically, they help to document, share, and spark conversations around design decisions as well as to streamline workflows that maximize consistency and save time. These objectives in turn mean that for many smaller organizations that do not have rapidly changing products, a complete design system with encoded patterns is often unnecessary. A 10-minute conversation in a small team to review a new design element can provide clarity and share approaches faster than a designer can write down all the thinking around it, let alone everyone finding time to reading about it. With this in mind, let's consider the factors affecting the appropriateness of a design system with patterns and components for a team or organization.

When to use a design system

Use a design system when

- There are so many people involved that conversations are inefficient or impossible

- There are other challenges to fluid conversations like teams working across time zones, parents leaving early to pick up kids, part-time employees, or limited times allocated to the project

- Handing over to another team, such as an agency building an inspirational pattern library for an in-house team

- Onboarding new employees quickly, so they can understand what's available, what decisions have been made in the past, and what the organization values

- You have many content contributors writing copy, developing images, editing videos, and curating content from diverse teams

- You have the time, skills, and resources to build a design system

- Names for UI patterns are undecided and causing confusion

- You want to have a single source of truth to ensure consistent design

If you decide that a few of the preceding factors apply to you and you want to build a design system, where do you start? Let's have a look.

Framing

Framing a design system can be useful to let people know how to engage with it; consider the context, audience, and purpose of the design system.

Context

You might need to establish whether your design system guidelines take a *practical* stance or an *inspirational* stance. A practical system prioritizes speed and functionality. You would use it as lightweight documentation, covering the bare minimum to jot decisions down, share code snippets, and reuse components. An inspirational system motivates team members to create beautiful products, surfacing brand values, and encouraging cohesion in the user experience, even at the expense of efficient and consistent development.[12]

---

[12]Read more about these approaches in Andy Clarke's article about "Designing Imaginative Style Guides" (`https://24ways.org/2016/designing-imaginative-style-guides/`).

Audience

Consider who will use your design system, including designers, developers, writers, third-party plug-in creators, teams from other companies within your company group, other agencies, and other government organizations. For example, Salesforce's Lightning Design System supports not only their internal contributors but anyone working on a custom application using the Salesforce platform,[13] which has far greater reach than their internal teams. Similarly, the U.S. Web Design System provides patterns and design principles for all government organizations across the United States.

Beyond the size and shape of teams using your design system, you'll need to think about their skills, tools, environments, and what tasks they might need to perform. For example, the Salesforce folk use rapid prototyping in the browser (`https://github.com/salesforce-ux/design-system-starter-kit`) to iterate quickly and test UI ideas. They describe this as being necessary to scaling their design process (`https://medium.com/salesforce-ux/the-salesforce-team-model-for-scaling-a-design-system-d89c2a2d404b`). On the other hand, the design team at Airbnb demand synced Sketch assets and React components (`https://airbnb.design/painting-with-code/`) and thus have an elaborate design system to handle this. One key aspect of their design system is Airbnb's React Sketch.app (`http://airbnb.io/react-sketchapp/`) that uses a shared system to keep React (code) and Sketch (design) assets perfectly in sync.

Purpose

While there may be many benefits to using a design system, establishing the primary purpose will give clarity to how to design your design system. Efficiency and speed in design and development might focus on

---

[13]Salesforce Developers, "Salesforce Platform," `https://developer.salesforce.com/platform`.

sharing vocabulary and integrating design and development processes. Consistency may mean facilitating reuse above all else.

Once you have this information in mind, it's time to gather buy in and spark interest in the design system. Most people can get behind a movement to improve the quality of a product, but committing time and resources to it can be another story. Framing the vision of the design system, what it will achieve, how it will be used, and how it will be developed can build awareness among affected parties, desire to contribute and engage with it, and knowledge of how to proceed. It can be useful to build a sense of urgency about the drivers for a design system ("if we don't do something now, at this rate our CSS will increase 10X by end of year, and page performance will suffer, losing a fifth of our customers for every second of lag introduced").

In order for people to grow the ability needed to use the design system well, you'll need to examine the workflow.

Workflows and design processes

At what point in the design and development process of a product will your team use the design system? How will they engage with it and grow it? Here are some examples of times a team might use a design system:

- Writing design specifications for a new feature to be developed. You can include the pattern to be used, linking to an existing reference and saving time.

- During design reviews. To settle a debate about the use of a particular pattern, you might refer to documented design decisions in the system.

- Prototyping or mocking up using existing design and code assets for patterns or components.

- Code testing.

  - Visual regression testing[14] ensures code changes don't affect designs over time. Learn more about testing with style guides (`https://tinnedfruit.com/articles/are-you-writing-legacy-css-code.html`).

  - Performance testing by measuring the size of style and script assets in your style guide as a proxy for site performance means you don't need to track your whole site.

  - For more details, check out Jim Newbery's comprehensive guide to pattern library testing (`https://tinnedfruit.com/articles/why-and-how-to-test-your-pattern-library.html`).

- For onboarding new employees, a design system might be an interesting insight into what the brand values and how processes work, so include your design system in onboarding documentation.

- During a *design share* where different designers in a team respectively showcase and discuss their new design work with the team. If you're running regular design shares, integrating a design system will slide into the process seamlessly. Any newly designed components that haven't existed before can be added to a "new" section of the design system. If it's never used more than twice, it's not really a "recurring solution," so it may not be worth documenting thoroughly or refining. When a new component is

---

[14]For a comprehensive list of resources on visual regression testing, see Visual Regression Testing (`https://visualregressiontesting.com/`).

used a few times or several similar components are created, they can undergo more thorough design and code reviews to refine a single component for reuse. Note that regular design shares can also identify inconsistencies if a "new" component is added where an existing one should have been reused. Read more about developing a process for making changes to patterns in Brad Frost's book *Atomic Design* (`http://atomicdesign.bradfrost.com/chapter-5/#making-changes-to-patterns`).

- Hand over. For example, design a mockup first and provide a `.sketch` file and a `.png` preview inside the design system but provide no code samples. Then a developer can build it out there in the library before using it in the product.

As we continue, we'll explore further how to optimize your design system for each of the preceding different touch points.

For some people, the word "processes" sends shivers up their spine, associating it with unwanted changes and burdensome overhead. This is what you want to avoid when integrating a design system into a team making products.

Pattern previews

Now we're getting to the guts of your design system. For each pattern, you'll need a preview or demo to show what it looks like so you and your team can recognize and find patterns quickly. The pattern itself needs to be visually distinct from the page that houses it. For example, previews in Culture Amp's Kaizen Design System include a checkerboard background style—like Photoshop's transparency grid—to distinguish the live component preview from the page it's inside, as shown in Figure 4-6.

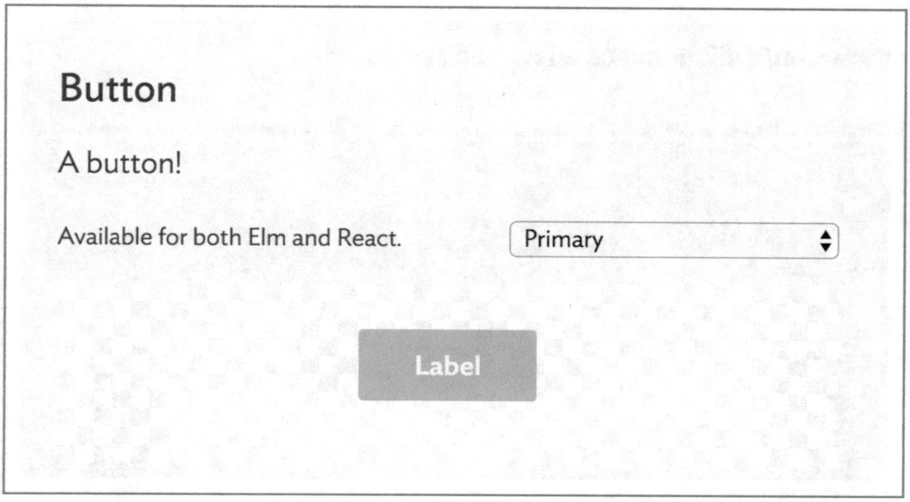

Figure 4-6. *Screenshot of Culture Amp's primary button*

To further illustrate the use of this grid background, Figure 4-7 shows Culture Amp's primary reversed button on a solid color background.

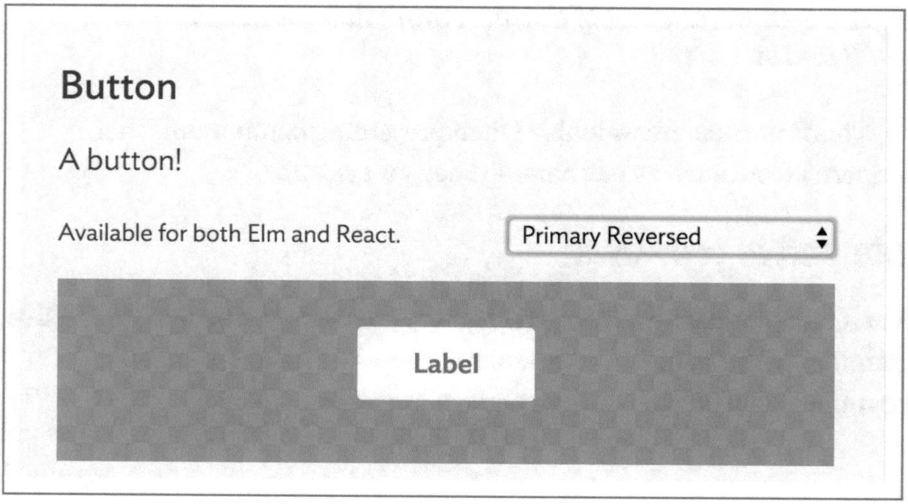

Figure 4-7. *Screenshot of Culture Amp's primary reversed button on a solid background*

Finally, for a full-width button, Figure 4-8 shows how a full-width button would fill the space on a small screen.

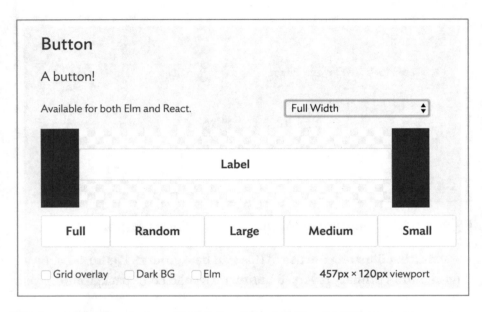

Figure 4-8. *Screenshot of Culture Amp's full-width button on a small screen*

This is particularly valuable when presenting components that concern layout such as nav bars, so keep an eye out.

Interactive previews

When combined with a living style guide, previews can be live, interactive examples of the pattern's component in action. Figure 4-9 shows an example of one of MailChimp's pattern previews.

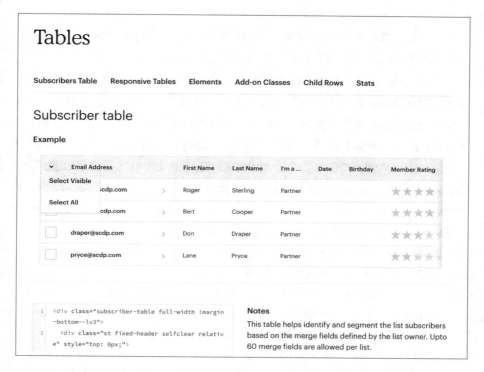

Figure 4-9. *Screenshot of MailChimp's Interactive Table Pattern*

In MailChimp's pattern library (`https://ux.mailchimp.com/ patterns`), you can interact with the patterns, so a dropdown in a table will actually drop down when you click it.

This approach provides the highest level of fidelity in illustrating how a pattern operates. This needs work from developers (unlike a static image), which means building the library is more than a tweak to an existing workflow without a design system, but an actual piece of work. This may or may not be feasible within your constraints, so it's something to bear in mind.

This approach is excellent for practical pattern libraries. It allows you to perform rapid prototyping in the browser. It also means you can more deeply understand the states and behavior of the element, such as seeing and feeling how hover styles appear and elements move when you interact.

Note   You might be familiar with prototyping using different levels of fidelity from a lo-fi sketch to a hi-fi interactive prototype to simulate real behavior. The main trade-offs are the speed you gain producing lo-fi prototypes vs. the realism you achieve with hi-fi prototypes. Each realistic detail removed from a prototype introduces a risk that it's an inaccurate test. Realism in your design system carries similar trade-offs where you may not convey as much information in a static image as you could with motion and interaction.

One challenge to this approach is writing enough code to make it genuinely interactive without having real data to fill a component or destinations for links. For example, if you wanted to present a notification component containing an image and realistic text with a link, you would need to really upload an image and create a working link to somewhere. You may need to write extra code to handle when a component that needs data, such as a data table component, doesn't have it (because it's presented in the design system) as well as when it does (in actual product usage). Similarly, if a form component normally submits data when you click the submit button, not having that data might blow up in your design system preview unless you take special care to handle that. You may also need to use dummy data, which can cause confusion about what's a part of the pattern and what's a part of the demo.

A shortcut to achieving interactive previews might be to link to code demos on the Internet, such as a Codepen for morphing buttons (`https://codepen.io/angeliastefani/pen/WOozVx`), if you cannot include your own interactive patterns.

Live markup and styling

Instead of an interactive example, however, you might include the markup and styling needed to present a pattern preview illustrating the core of the pattern, but leave out interactive details that would integrate it on a real product page. For example, FutureLearn's feed item (`https://design-system.futurelearn.com/molecules/feed-item`) in Figure 4-10 shows you how a feed item looks on mobile, tablet, laptop, and desktop devices, but while in the design system you cannot follow the links in the feed item or add the feed item to your favorites.

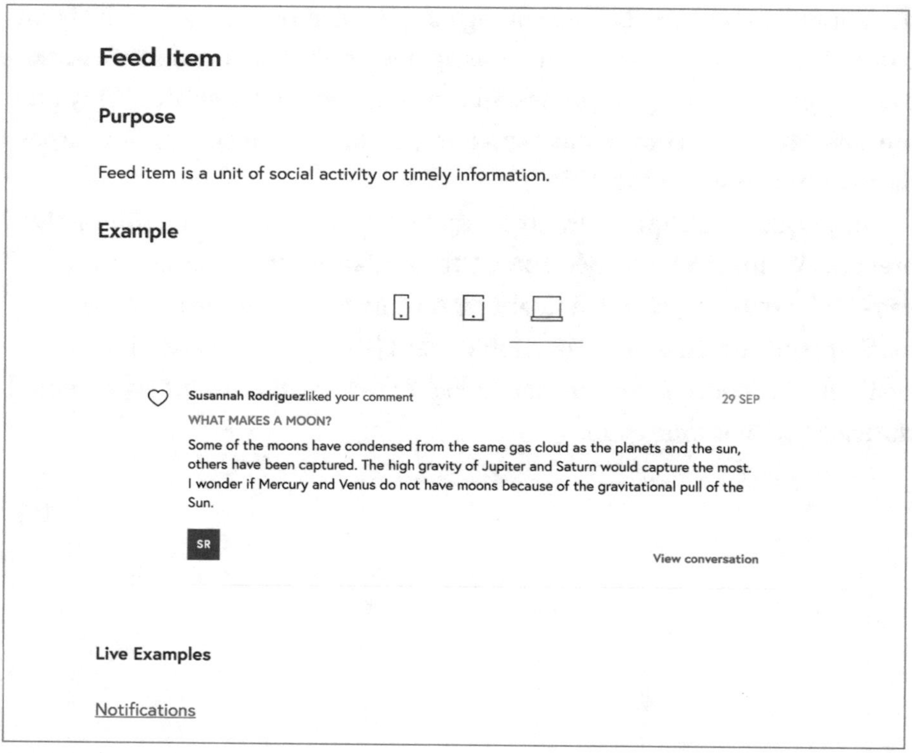

Figure 4-10. *Screenshot of FutureLearn's feed item preview and link to live examples*

If you follow the live examples link, however, it will take you to an instance of the component in use within the app.

FutureLearn's "feed item" looks like our activity feed pattern in action. They describe it in this way:

Feed item is a unit of social activity or timely information.

It contains a distinguishing element (an avatar or an icon), heading, and content. Optionally it can include a secondary heading, metadata, and user actions.

In addition to a single example, they describe modifiers—compact, indented, alt, and bordered. As you can see, this is a little more precise than our abstract activity feed, giving you detail about using it with visual content such as avatars or icons. Seeing how individuals and organizations execute patterns can give you fascinating insights into their flexibility and limitations, such as how a distinguishing avatar can make each feed item more interesting and valuable.

As another example of live markup and styling without an interactive preview, Walmart's web style guide (`http://walmartlabs.github.io/web-style-guide/`) shows a flyout pattern using the pattern's actual markup and styling to present each variant (flying out in each of four available directions). You can see in Figure 4-11, each variant is presented statically in their final state.

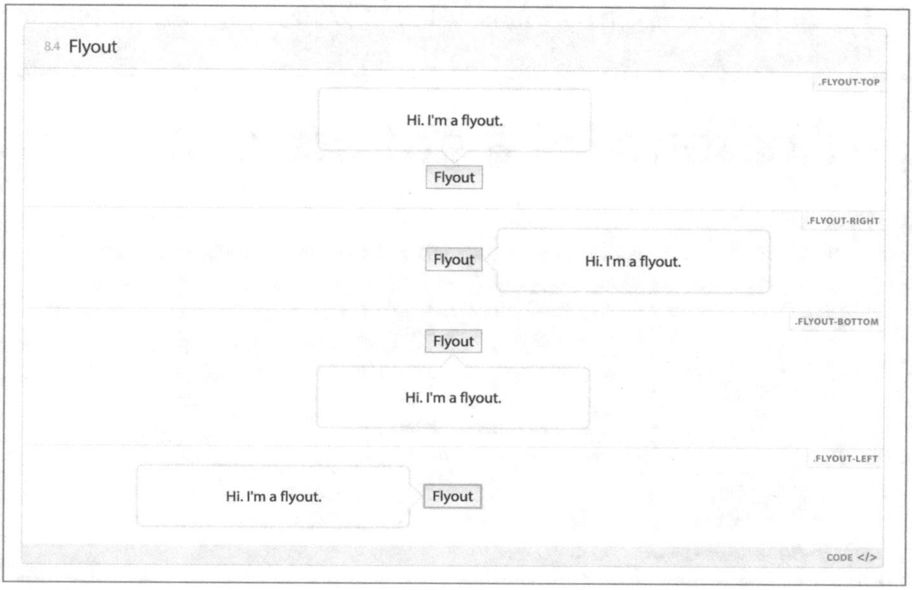

Figure 4-11. *Screenshot of Walmart's Flyout pattern*

This approach lets you see all variations of a pattern side by side. If you make any style changes, you'll see how it affects each version. The downside is that it might introduce some ambiguity. Can a flyout be trigged by hover alone or must you tap the toggle button?

Static images, animations, and videos

To create a preview or demo, one option is that you show an image of it without any real code behind it. Material Design's notification (`https://material.io/design/platform-guidance/android-notifications.html#anatomy-of-a-notification`), for example, provides a static image using example apps and videos for animated elements.

171

Figure 4-12 shows a static image using an example app for the preview.

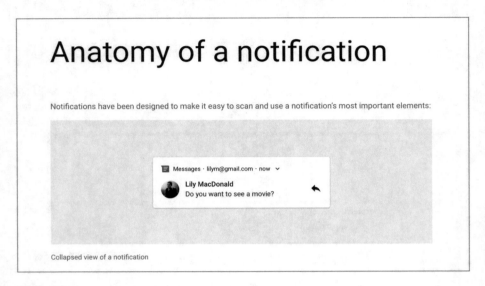

Figure 4-12. *Screenshot of Material Design's notification static example image*

Figure 4-13 shows a video where a static image would be insufficient to convey the concept.

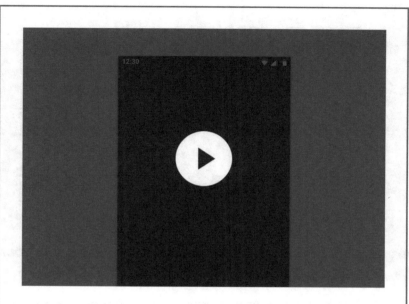

When a notification arrives, an icon usually appears in the status bar. This signals to the user that there's something to see in the notification drawer.

Figure 4-13. *Screenshot of Material Design's notification video*

Interestingly, Material Design used to also have abstract mockups like the notification skeleton shown in Figure 4-14, but no longer includes any previews in this style. This might be a hint that it was insufficient to convey the idea.

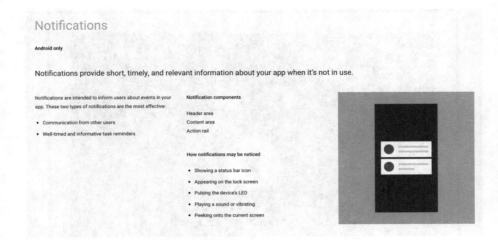

Figure 4-14. *Screenshot of Material Design's abstract notification visual*

Using static images and pre-recorded videos for previews means that you need not write any code and more people may be able to easily update your design system without spending time coding.

Additionally, it makes it possible to demonstrate larger and more interactive elements within a design system that might otherwise be tricky. For example, Lightning's Loading guidelines (`www.lightningdesignsystem.com/guidelines/loading/`) show loading spinners and what they call "stencils" (a.k.a. skeleton screens), illustrated in Figure 4-15.

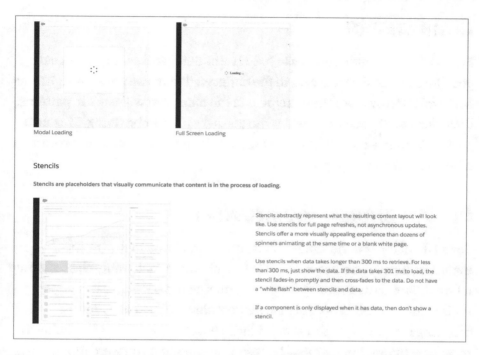

Figure 4-15. *Screenshot of Lightning's loading spinners and stencils*

If they had presented a real stencil to preview the pattern, you'd only have a split second or so to see it before it loaded the full data, which limits the illustrative ability of it. Similarly, imagine chasing down an infinite scrolling page just to see the loading spinner.

This approach is excellent for inspirational pattern libraries.

The trade-off, however, is that more time may be spent on content creation whenever the tiniest detail changes and the preview assets need to be updated.

Code assets

For a practical pattern library to help teams achieve their product goals, you can provide direct access to the code needed to use patterns right next to them. To truly tailor these helpers to the team that will use the patterns, however, you'll need to consider the tasks they might be doing. This next section includes more code than the rest of the book. If that's not your cup of tea, feel free to skip over it.

Prototyping in the browser

For a UI engineer or designer that wants to prototype in the browser, including a code snippet of raw HTML with functional, utility classes would let them rapidly assemble patterns together in the browser's developer tools elements inspector. Further, for complex interactive patterns, exposing JavaScript methods to initialize functions would let UI engineers prototype interactive features. For example, imagine you were prototyping with a JavaScript-driven tooltip. Given this tooltip HTML code snippet:

```
<button
class="btn btn-primary"
data-toggle="tooltip"
title="Add item to favorites">
  <span
  class="glyphicon glyphicon-heart"
  aria-hidden="true">
  </span>
</button>
```

You could mock up an icon button, but you'd be unable to produce a tooltip on hover. If the design system also included $('[data-toggle="tooltip"]').tooltip(), you could initialize the tooltip in your prototype and have it behave like a normal one.

Writing code

Your design system might also provide boilerplate code to be used directly from a design system in the final code base. In this case, your code snippets need to be in the format that your code base uses, such as template processor like Slim[15] or Haml.[16] For example:

```
.activity-feed
  .activity-feed-event
    h1.activity-feed-event-name Name verb noun
    small.activity-feed-event-date M minutes ago
    p.activity-feed-event-description
      Paragraph describing event
    a.btn.btn-primary.activity-feed-event-share
      Share call to action
```

Further, if a component requires a "presenter," you can provide that code as well. A presenter might show repeating elements like each feed item in an activity feed for a set of feed items by calling one presenter code snippet. For example:

```
<div class="activity-feed">
  <%= ActivityFeed.new(events, user, options).markup %>
</div>
```

Finally, if there are variants, show those too. In this example, you can add activity-feed--featured to style the feed differently for more important content:

```
<div class="activity-feed activity-feed--featured">
  <%= ActivityFeed.new(events, user, options).markup %>
</div>
```

---

[15]"Slim," http://slim-lang.com/.
[16]"Haml," http://haml.info/.

Converting design elements to code

In addition to patterns, design systems will often extend the elements of living style guides and brand guidelines that help makers build products efficiently. Icons, colors, typography, logos, and fonts, for example, will be included in a manner that helps developers use them in their workflows, even though they're visual elements rather than patterns *per se*.

To weave these elements into workflows, design systems often include the following foundational design guidance.

- Icons:

    - Names to reference them in code, such as an `icon-heart` produce a heart icon from an icon image sprite.[17]

    - Accessibility usage, such as adding `aria-label=""` to describe unlabeled icon buttons and when to use `aria-hidden="true"` to hide icons from screen readers where a label would provide redundant information on a labeled icon button. Alternatively, you might add a `<title>` element to an SVG icon to describe the visual content.

    - Utilities for sizing, coloring, etc., such as `.icon` `.icon-small` `.icon-brand-red` `.icon-heart` to indicate a small, red heart icon.

    - Sprite preparation, such as a script to run to collate existing and new icons into a single sprite image for serving quickly to users' browsers.

---

[17]Mozilla Developer Network, "Implementing image sprites in CSS," `https://developer.mozilla.org/en-US/docs/Web/CSS/CSS_Images/Implementing_image_sprites_in_CSS`.

- Colors:

    - Brand colors in different formats, such as hex values (#ff0000) or `rgba(255, 0, 0, 0.8)`.

    - Sass variables and functions, for example, `$state-danger-bg: lighten($brand-danger, 25%);`.

    - Appropriate text colors on different background colors that are legible and aesthetically pleasing, meeting accessibility needs such as contrast requirements.

- Typography:

    - Vertical rhythm[18] and typography scale specification in Sass variables,[19] for example, `h1 { font-size: $type-scale(3); }`.

- Logos:

    - How to reference SVG logo images, for example, `<svg class="logo"><use xlink:href="path/to/logo.svg#lockup"></use></svg>` or in React `<Logo />`.[20]

    - Class names to indicate which color and arrangement of the logo to use, for example, `<svg class="logo logo-reverse logo-stacked"> ... </svg>` for a stacked, reversed logo on a solid fill background.

---

[18]Shelly Wilson, "4 Simple Steps to Vertical Rhythm," `http://typecast.com/blog/4-simple-steps-to-vertical-rhythm`.

[19]David Khourshid, "Aesthetic Sass 3: Typography and Vertical Rhythm," `https://scotch.io/tutorials/aesthetic-sass-3-typography-and-vertical-rhythm`.

[20]To learn more, see Creating an SVG Icon System with React (`https://css-tricks.com/creating-svg-icon-system-react/`) by Sarah Drasner.

- Fonts:

  - Font stacks including the main brand font as well as fall back fonts, for example, `font-family: 'Crimson Text', 'Lora', serif;`

Design assets

To use a design system for design tasks, you'll likely need to know color values in different formats, like hexadecimal (#), RGB (Red, Green, Blue), or HSL (Hue, Saturation, Lightness). For example, see Shopify's Polaris Color Palette (`https://polaris.shopify.com/design/colors#section-color-palette`). Figure 4-16 shows the palette presented in the Hex format.

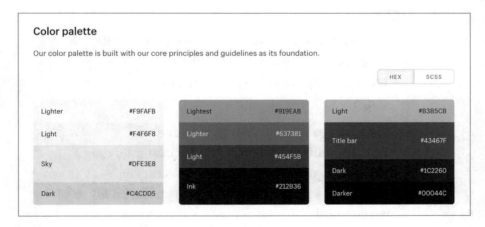

Figure 4-16. *Screenshot of Shopify's Polaris Hex colors*

Figure 4-17 shows the palette presented in SCSS (a CSS pre-processor) functions.

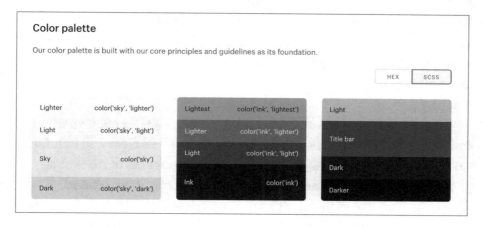

Figure 4-17. *Screenshot of Shopify's Polaris SCSS colors*

You'll also likely need other standard information (often found in branding guidelines) like display and body font faces, and swatch files for design applications, such as Adobe Swatch Exchange files (`.ase`) for Illustrator and other Adobe products.

This is also a handy place to link directly to other design asset files like icon SVGs and UI source files like `.sketch` or `.psd` files or wireframing and prototyping assets like Axure or Omnigraffle files. That said, it's also a great place for design assets that do not require design specific tools and licenses for folk other than designers in the organization, like public relations professionals. You might include high-resolution exported images and slide deck templates.

For an example of design assets in design systems, check out U.S. Web Design System's designer resources (`https://designsystem. digital.gov/documentation/designers/`) or Shopify's Polaris UI Kit and other resources (`https://polaris.shopify.com/resources/resources`).

181

Writing and content

As your patterns and components will undoubtedly include text, the library is a good place to link to or include editorial style resources, especially as they pertain to digital products. For example, a traditional editorial style guide may not mention whether to use "Title Case" or "Sentence case" on buttons or how to localize interfaces into different languages.

When developing your internal library patterns, your copywriter can write good defaults into all the components like a clear and helpful validation feedback messages in your form components to streamline good copy practices and ensure interface microcopy is not missed.

For an example of this, check out Shopify's Polaris Content Grammar and Mechanics section (`https://polaris.shopify.com/content/grammar-and-mechanics#basics`).

Documenting patterns or components

In practice, rather than creating pattern libraries and documenting patterns from scratch, individual organizations create design systems that encode patterns with a specific visual design language in component libraries with documentation. Sometimes they link to tools and resources that speak to the broader pattern but rarely do they describe an abstract pattern; they describe a specific execution of a pattern in their specific domain.

Nathan Curtis suggests that "Our Community, not Companies, Should Build Pattern Libraries."[21] He also suggests that most organizations would only need to craft their own patterns (rather than components) for "the most essential patterns unique to their customer experience," such as

---

[21]Nathan Curtis, "Patterns ≠ Components," `https://medium.com/eightshapes-llc/patterns-components-2ce778cbe4e8`.

"A bank's pattern to move money from one account to another." In many cases, the product's unique value proposition can be encapsulated by this one, most essential pattern.

When it comes to creating and documenting new patterns in your design system, I suggest focusing your efforts on that one most essential pattern to your business, or the patterns that cause the most contention in your organization. Popular areas for arguments among digital practitioners outside the scope of their unique business include: when to use a link or a button,[22] when to use target="blank"[23] to force a link to open in a new tab, and what cursor for a button or link.[24]

For more information on documenting UI patterns in your design system, Nathan Curtis again provides us with an excellent series on Documenting Components (`https://medium.com/eightshapes-llc/documenting-components-9fe59b80c015`).

Extra design system features

To help navigate the design system, you could provide an overview, a table of contents, or an autocomplete search as we saw in Chapter 2. Figure 4-18 shows an example of autocomplete search to find components regardless of the section they live in.

---

[22]Marcy Sutton, "Links vs. Buttons in Modern Web Applications," `https://marcysutton.com/links-vs-buttons-in-modern-web-applications`.

[23]Chris Coyier, "When to use target="_blank"," `https://css-tricks.com/use-target_blank/`.

[24]Roman Komarov, "Correct Cursor on Active Elements," `www.kizu.ru/cursor-pointer/`.

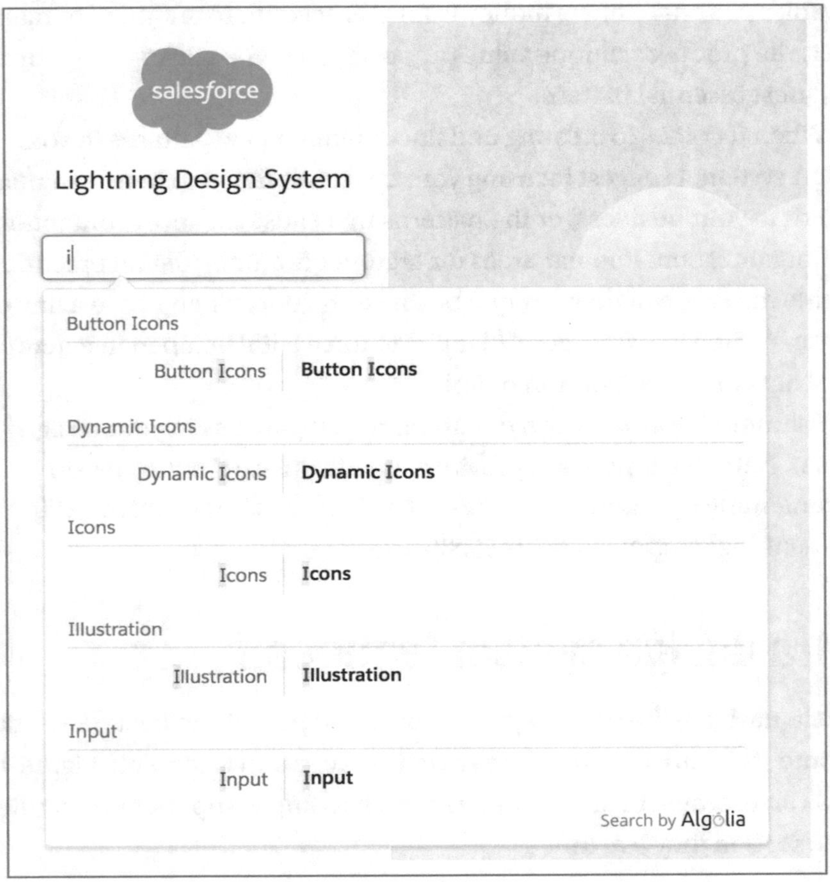

Figure 4-18. *Screenshot of Lightning Design System's autocomplete search*

As you can see in Figure 4-19, Walmart's style guide includes clickable anchors next to each example's heading so you can link directly to a pattern on a long page.

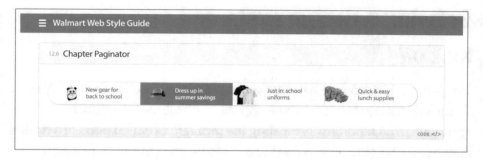

Figure 4-19. *Screenshot of Walmart's Chapter Paginator pattern*

Using this method, you can include links directly in project management tools for describing upcoming feature specifications or to share in discussions over email or instant messaging. This is especially useful for distributed and remote teams.

A common enhancement you'll find in mature front-end style guides is a button to "copy to clipboard" to copy code snippets, as shown in Figure 4-20.

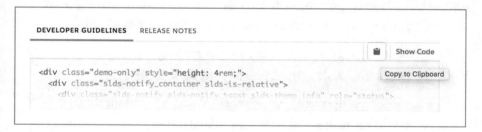

Figure 4-20. *Screenshot of Lightning Design System developer guidelines including a copy to clipboard button*

Growing a design system
Kick off

How do you kick off a new design system? One method is to use Nathan Curtis's design system worksheet approach.[25] This uses a workshop approach to collaboratively tackling the problem of which parts of a design system to solve (including whether a design system is even a priority), all of the products or digital "properties" (such as a web site, web app, social media presence) to consider, and the people needed to make it all happen—the individual contributors, influential leads, and distant leaders like directors. This approach *builds consensus* while actually solving the issues of how to build a design resource.

Alternatively, to instigate conversations, you might start with the compelling interface inventory[26] to screenshot and collect all the different, inconsistent interface elements actually in use in your products. This identifies patterns already in use and the scope of the work ahead, but may also be used to highlight the severity of inconsistencies in your products. If your priority is in improving consistency, this is a useful starting point.

Once you've identified all the pieces, you can start to clarify

- Which patterns exist that are successfully solving problems. This is the basis of your design system.

- Which components are *almost* solving a problem that could be addressed with a standard pattern.

- Where there's wild variation in behavior and usage of components.

---

[25]Nathan Curtis, "Picking Parts, Products & People," https://medium.com/eightshapes-llc/picking-parts-products-people-a06721e81742.

[26]Brad Frost, "Interface Inventory," http://bradfrost.com/blog/post/interface-inventory/.

- What's actively having a negative impact. We'll look at anti-patterns in Chapter 5.

- Where there are special snowflakes that are never reused. Sometimes these represent unique, delightful, or signature experiences. Other times they highlight unnecessary customizations that could be removed.

Use these to discuss your product's UI patterns with your team and start naming them.

Assembly

Once you have a rough draft of all your patterns, you can work on presenting them. An effective design system is informed by diverse contributors. That is, imagine how a designer might feel about developers using a design system when it is ugly and untouched by the designers that would have the skills to ensure their usability. Likewise, imagine how a developer might feel about being forced to depend on a UI Kit that's constantly out of sync with production styles where some elements are out of date and some aren't ready to be rolled out yet. As such, it's necessary that all parties using the system can contribute to and effectively use it. Some options for storage might include

- A wiki: While it might lack requisite tech details, anyone can write to it.

- A Dropbox folder: It might lack versioning, but could be easily accessed and easily include a mix of design and development assets like Photoshop or Sketch source files and exports as well as code specifications.

- A code repository: This might ensure versions are controlled, but be inaccessible to folk that don't know how to read or write code. This could be augmented with a social coding interface like GitHub, where anyone can leave comments, raise issues, and attach files.

- An internal web site with commenting features: Tech folk may directly build the site itself, while non-tech folk can write info about the patterns on the site.

Versioning

The designs, code, and underlying UI patterns will change over time. It's not always possible to roll out every relevant change at the same time, such as moving a web site from one front-end framework to another, more powerful framework. As such, your design system might have multiple versions: one using the old framework for most patterns and one using the new framework for enhanced interactions. Like any software package, you could use semantic versioning (`https://semver.org/`) to denote patches, minor changes, and major breaking changes in your design system.

For example, Walmart's style guide suggests the "Display Price" component, shown in Figure 4-21, has been deprecated in favor of the more generic "Price" component.

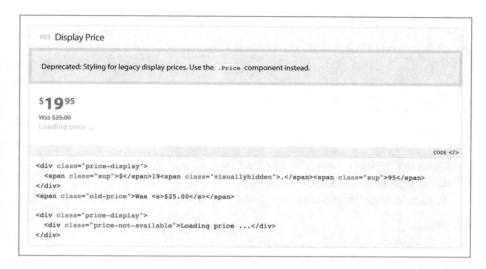

Figure 4-21. *Screenshot of Walmart's Display Price component with deprecation warning*

Figure 4-22 shows the "Price" component.

Figure 4-22. *Screenshot of Walmart's Price component with far more detail and variations*

You'll notice with UI frameworks such as Bootstrap that you can still use and find documentation for older versions.[27] The more people using your library, the more care you'll need to take supporting the constraints they're working with that might limit them from keeping up with you.

---

[27]"BootstrapDocs," https://bootstrapdocs.com/.

Serving assets

If you've created a public-facing design system as part of product web site, be sure to avoid delivering unnecessary code to their browsers. For example, only serve the extra code needed to present the library to people visiting that library page instead of shipping it with the rest of your style and script assets for regular site visitors using the product. For the most part, if you're using neatly encapsulated components, you won't require much additional code. Effective code splitting and delivery can also help.

Tools

In your library, link to any tools that help people assess, use, and refine patterns. For example, try these:

- Color contrast, legibility, and color blindness testing tools

- Accessibility testing tools

- Performance testing or otherwise tracking the weight of files (such as your CSS) over time or number of files included (such as number of icons or font files used)

- Readability testing tools, such as Hemingway app for highlighting reading levels and clear language

- Helpers, such as Lonely Planet's Closest Color tool (https://rizzo.lonelyplanet.com/styleguide/design-elements/ui-colours) for pasting in a hex value and returning the closest UI color in their design system as a hex value or Sass variable

- Extra assets like a Sketch UI kit or React components[28]

---

[28]See, for example, Shopify's Polaris design system resource page (https://polaris.shopify.com/resources/resources).

191

Evolution

No doubt everyone will love your design system and want to be involved. Okay, this might be an optimistic view in some cases, but if your design system is ticking along smoothly, you might find more good ideas pouring in than you have time to process and address. You can triage all of the suggestions using a standard "issue tracker" like GitHub's issues or even a customer support tool.

When changes are made to your design system, you'll want to share everything and let people know what's changed. This is an opportunity to celebrate progress so be sure to call out the effort people have made and how valuable that contribution is to the organization's mission. Following another programming habit, you might use a "change log" to keep a log of changes made between design system versions, and share "release notes" to highlight the significant differences, including screenshots of what's new.

For a list of design system resources, see the suggested reading in the Appendix.

Summary

Design systems include all manner of design communication documentation, such as internal pattern libraries, public pattern libraries, brand guides, editorial style guides, design guidelines, front-end style guides, and component libraries.

We've reviewed the varied uses of design systems and pattern libraries, especially for their abilities to clarify design decisions.

Finally, we've seen *when* a design system might be an appropriate tool to use (usually when design reviews aren't possible).

CHAPTER 5

Anti-patterns and dark patterns

Healthy skepticism is often the best way to glean the value of what's being presented—challenge it; prove it wrong, if you can. That creates engagement, which is the key to understanding.

—David Allen, *Getting Things Done*

What are anti-patterns?

Anti-patterns are recurring solutions that create more problems than they solve. On the surface, they may seem appealing as solutions to your design problems, but dig a little deeper and you'll find there's more pain than promise. As with the three ingredients of a UI pattern we saw in Chapter 1, here are the details of an anti-pattern:

- A named "solution" or approach describing *what* the anti-pattern does, including the **symptoms**, where there are more bad consequences than good.

- A **tempting reason** *why* you might be seduced into using the anti-pattern, including the user problem it sought to address.

© Diana MacDonald 2019
D. MacDonald, *Practical UI Patterns for Design Systems,*
https://doi.org/10.1007/978-1-4842-4938-3_5

- Some **missing context** for *when* it could have been viable. This usually suggests alternative, suitable UI patterns.

- Some **recovery steps** explaining *how* to recover, including alternative patterns that exist and are successful. Sometimes, there are preventative measures too.

Let's look at an example. **Mystery meat navigation** describes links that do not have a clear destination. The user needs to hover over the link to reveal the link's destination or follow it blindly, making your product harder to understand and operate. Like mystery meat—processed meats with unidentified sources—mystery meat navigation is clear to the creator but not to the consumer.

A common example of mystery meat navigation is the infamous "click here" link. These poorly labeled links are confusing when read out of context, for example, by a screen reader or someone scanning a page quickly for specific information. The user is forced to hover over or touch and hold the link for the browser to show the link target, and even then, a URL doesn't explain the content of the link target. Another example of mystery meat navigation is unlabeled icons. The symptoms of mystery meat navigation include decreased click confidence, wayfinding challenges, longer task completion times, and potentially abandonment.

Anti-pattern names typically take on a more humorous or memorable name to call out the absurdity of using it and draw attention to its flaws. Otherwise you might (reasonably) refer to mystery meat navigation links as "click here" links, hiding their nefarious nature. By having a sharper name, you can recognize its true nature.

When crafting link text, it might be tempting to use "click here" because it's a common staple of the early Web and it's explicit about what you want the user to do next. It's especially tempting when you start a sentence with "To learn more": "To learn more about bees, click here." Instead, you could link the subject itself, for example, "Learn more about bees."

Similarly, it might be tempting to use unlabeled icons to save space, reduce visual clutter, and avoid translating text. One time when it might be worth keeping the unlabeled icons is when you have extremely experienced, highly engaged users using a limited number of unlabeled icons with high frequency. For example, a Facebook user that checks in every day may not need labels for the primary navigation items they use habitually. Instead of unlabeled icons, you might add labels to icons or replace them with text alone.

Why care about anti-patterns?

Learning anti-patterns helps you recognize them more quickly and learn how to untangle yourself from one that's already in use. When uncovering anti-patterns, it's useful to *assume positive intent* by the designer using the anti-pattern in attempting to solve their problem. It's rare that people set out to create impenetrable user interfaces and anti-patterns can be deceptively appealing.

There will be at least some appeal to the anti-pattern solution:

- The approach is useful in the short term but will have negative consequences in the long term. The long-term consequences might seem acceptable or be overlooked.

- The approach might be intended as a stop-gap solution, but lingers for unexpected reasons, such as the development team being out sick delaying additional work.

- The solution would be suitable in a slightly different context, but it's been mismatched to the situation at hand.

- There are other forces at play outside of the design problem, such as management issues (like the mythical man month we saw earlier).

Patterns may also suggest shortcomings in your environment like the technology available. For example, displaying a login form might be unnecessary in an iOS app that uses a thumb print to authenticate a known user. The thumb print authentication makes the username and password fields of a login form redundant. Without thumb print access, however, the login form pattern would be suitable.

Uncovering the failure mode of an anti-pattern helps in understanding why interfaces fail and may assist in seeing problems in advance when new design trends come around.

Note   UI anti-patterns aren't just bad UI design. Unlike poor UI choice, anti-patterns *seem* like good solutions on the surface. Further, the scope of the problem in an anti-pattern is often larger than just the UI: the root cause of an anti-pattern might be the governance and business processes that surround how a web site component is updated. UI anti-patterns develop from a combination of people, parts, and processes.

Even when a bad pattern falls out of favor (owing to its many drawbacks), that doesn't mean it's *never* the right solution; only that the odds are lower. Even a good UI pattern can become an anti-pattern if its solution depends on a specific context, like an era of web design, conventions, and technology, and it's misapplied to a new and different context.

Anti-pattern: Hamburger basement

As a UI pattern, this was originally called the **hamburger menu**: three lines indicating a "hamburger" button in the top-left or top-right corner of an interface that opened and closed a menu, usually containing links to different parts of a product.

Giving it a more ridiculous name that highlights the flaws of it, the **hamburger basement** anti-pattern stashes options away behind the hamburger button leading to fewer people using them.

Figure 5-1 shows a hamburger button.

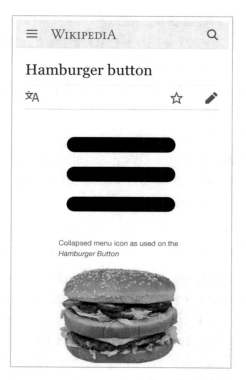

Figure 5-1. *Screenshot of Wikipedia's article about the hamburger button on a page with a hamburger button*

The problem that this anti-pattern was attempting to solve was managing primary navigation on tiny screens. In the pursuit of prioritizing content to create an immersive experience and balancing this pursuit with access to primary navigation, the community sought to shrink navigation down to one thumb-sized link so it's there when you need it but stays out of the way. Unfortunately this creates other issues:

- Decreased **discoverability**: It's harder for users to stumble upon other great features in your product.

- Decreased **location signalling**: Users will find it harder to identify where they are if you remove another source of you-are-here navigation.[1]

- Increased **cost of interaction**: The menu requires an additional tap to access it compared to immediately accessible links.

- Increased **thumb stretching**: Hamburger menu icons are kept in the hardest-to-reach locations on tiny screens for your users' thumbs.

- A form of **mystery meat navigation**: Users won't know what's in the menu behind the icon until they tap it.

- Increased **analysis paralysis**: A long list of links in the menu with little context about their destinations makes it hard to select an item. If the user chooses the wrong link, they need to start the time-consuming process of trial-and-error tapping each link behind the hamburger button again.

- Decreased **click confidence**: Users hesitate with unlabeled icons.

- Increased **context switching**: It can be unclear where the menu came from and how it relates to the current page, especially if it appears suddenly without a transition.

---

[1]Susan Farrell, "Navigation: You Are Here," `www.nngroup.com/articles/navigation-you-are-here/`.

- Increased **confusion across platforms**: Users don't understand or recognize the hamburger at all on desktop web sites and might find the icon in unusual locations on native iOS apps where the platform reserves the top-left corner for existing navigation elements like "back" arrows or "exit" crosses. In this case, the solution used doesn't fit the context.

As it turns out, hidden navigation cuts discoverability in half and destroys engagement.[2] Beyond the hamburger basement, this gives us clues about what to look for in the future when new "patterns" arise that turn out to be anti-patterns. If you see hidden navigation elements leading to poor navigation within your product, you will be able to recognize this familiar trap and nip it in the bud.

It's not all bad news for hamburger menus though. To change a "basement" to a "menu," there are some steps you can take:

- Only keep secondary navigation elements or infrequently accessed features in the hamburger menu, such as about pages, history, settings, permissions, copyright, privacy policies, sponsorship, advertising, affiliates, disclaimers, cookie policies, licensing, help, security, terms, and so on.

- For secondary navigation elements included in a hamburger menu, examine the information architecture of your navigation menu to establish clear labels, categories, and order to your links.

---

[2]Luke Wroblewski, "Obvious Always Wins," www.lukew.com/ff/entry.asp?1945, April 2015.

- Extract primary navigation elements from the hamburger menu and expose them in the main interface instead of hidden behind a click. For this you might use, for example, a bottom tab nav bar with the current nav item clearly selected.

- Move the menu button to a thumb-friendly region.

- Aggressively prioritize content so that primary navigation is correctly identified and easily accessible. The hamburger basement can be a clue that you've failed to prioritize as aggressively as possible.

- Increase clickability signifiers like surrounding the hamburger icon with a border to look like a button or giving it a "menu" label.

- Label your icons.

- Avoid use on desktop.

- Increase content links.

Figure 5-2 shows one alternative to the hamburger basement.

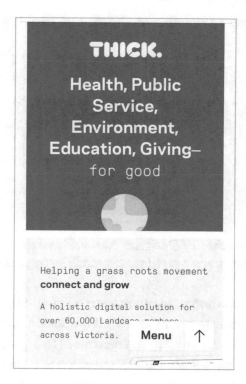

Figure 5-2. *Screenshot of Thick studio using a fixed "Menu" button in the thumb zone*

These steps don't necessarily mean you will completely kill off the hamburger menu, only that you can make it less of a dank, scary basement by mitigating some of the worst effects of it.

What else can we learn from the hamburger basement anti-pattern? In the hamburger basement, we can see some of the basic tenets of UX violated. When considering new UI patterns, we must be on the look out to identify the trade-offs we're making when we employ them. Given how undiscoverable the hamburger menu is, what makes us think sideways scrolling nav will be any better?

Figure 5-3 shows an example of a horizontal scrolling navigation bar.

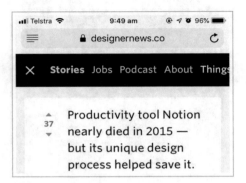

Figure 5-3. *Screenshot of Designer News where tapping the hamburger button reveals a sideways scrolling nav bar*

Similar to the hamburger menu pattern and hamburger basement anti-pattern, the overflow menu[3] has been branded a junk drawer.[4] This example shows us a similar tempting reasons to use a "solution" that brings more bad consequences than good when used in a context that doesn't fit.

What are dark patterns?

Another way that UI design can go awry is through the use of **dark patterns** or **evil design** (sometimes referred to as "black hat UX"): deceptive patterns that benefit the creator more than the user. They often persuade users into performing an action they didn't intend, such as

---

[3]Daniel Burka, "Stop the overuse of overflow menus," `https://medium.freecodecamp.org/stop-the-overuse-of-overflow-menus-5caa4b54e843`, July 2016.

[4]Jakob Nielsen and Page Laubheimer, "Top 10 Application-Design Mistakes," `www.nngroup.com/articles/top-10-application-design-mistakes/`, February 2019.

subscribing to a long contract with hidden fees. Sometimes they dissuade people from performing their intended action, such as unsubscribing. Commonly, the use of dark patterns is seen as being in pursuit of the bottom line—getting the sale no matter the cost to the user.

Design, by its nature, is used to communicate with and persuade people. Dark patterns, however, deceive people to achieve that goal.

Note   To learn more about dark patterns and the gray area, check out:

- Dark Patterns (`https://darkpatterns.org/`)
- Evil By Design (`http://evilbydesign.info/`)

Manipulinks and Confirmshamers

A manipulink is a link with manipulative link text. The term combines "manipulative" and "link." Unlike links with well-crafted microcopy that is precise and concrete, manipulinks make users feel bad by forcing them to click a link with irrelevant text to actual the task: dismissing a notification or modal (they usually replace "cancel," "close," or "dismiss" as link text).

The irrelevant link text requires the users to make an identity statement about their values aligning with some negative quality like, "No thanks, I prefer not making money," "No, I prefer paying full price," or "No thanks, I don't like cute babies."[5]

---

[5]"confirmshaming," `http://confirmshaming.tumblr.com/image/161394731642`.

Figure 5-4 shows an example of a manipulink.

Figure 5-4. *Screenshot of Gmail's dismissal link microcopy that says, "I don't want smarter email"*

Manipulinks are sometimes called

- "declineshamers" because they're often used to decline an offer

- "confirmshamers" as they ask users to confirm something potentially shameful about themselves to remove the obstacle

- "painful buttons" to make the opt-out button less passive and more painful to users

Confirmshamers frequently appear on "exit-intent pop-ups," which are modals that pop up when a user indicates their intent to leave by moving their mouse toward the close button of a tab or back button of a browser. These are used in a few different ways:

- If the organization identifies a user as a shopper needing further incentive to make a decision, they may offer the user a discount on their purchase or use principles like scarcity and urgency to push the user over the line ("Only 5 items left!", "Offer ends in 3 days!").

- If the organization identifies the user as needing more information, they then attempt to offer more assistance such as live chat with customer support to address their concerns, particularly on e-commerce checkout pages.

- Failing all of that, the organization may settle for lead generation and attempt to capture your email address or social media accounts to market to you more later.

Before the user can leave, however, they must click a negatively worded link on that pop-up.

On the surface, manipulinks might seem like an effective use of compelling microcopy to increase conversions. As Kate Meyer and Kim Flaherty at Nielsen Norman Group point out, however, the short-term increase in leads might not be worth the long-term impact of lower Net Promoter Scores, negative brand perception, and loss of credibility and users' trust.[6]

As a label for a control, these manipulinks even fail at the basic task of describing what clicking the link will do: will it dismiss the modal or automatically email all my contacts that I prefer dumb email? The link text gives no clue about its actual behavior. Using this link text alone, a user with an assistive device like a screen reader may find it challenging to figure out how to operate the modal, to close it and return to their original task.

Beyond the bottom line, this dark pattern risks putting words in someone's mouth, encouraging negative self-talk that can affect mental health.[7]

To wind your way back from a manipulink, you might consider Copyhackers' opt-out boxes with consequences.[8] In addition to including a

---

[6]Kate Moran and Kim Flaherty, "Stop Shaming Your Users for Micro Conversions," www.nngroup.com/articles/shaming-users/.

[7]healthdirect, "Self talk," www.healthdirect.gov.au/self-talk.

[8]Joanna Wiebe, "Choices, Consequences and the Reason Every Pop-Up Box Needs 2 Buttons: Opt In, and Opt Out," https://copyhackers.com/2015/05/choices-consequences-opt-in-boxes/.

subscribe button in a newsletter signup pattern as we saw in
Chapter 2, Copyhackers suggest using an explicit opt-out link so users make
a conscious decision to accept the consequences of opting out rather than
deferring or delaying the decision by dismissing the question. By using the
phrase "No, I reject the persuasion guide," they are offering their users a
clearly expressed action that accurately describes what the user is *doing*.

Tip   There's a whole Tumblr about confirmshaming (`http://`
`confirmshaming.tumblr.com/`).

Design smells

**A bad smell or a code smell is a term commonly used in the software
development community to describe symptoms in a product that**
possibly indicate a deeper problem. To borrow the concept, **design smells**
are design issues that possibly indicate a deeper problem. You might think
of them as the smoke you see before you spot the fire. If you don't find the
fire and put it out in time, your whole product might go up in flames. On
the other hand, while design smells *might* indicate a deeper problem, they
might also be traced back to nothing sinister at all. Your smoke might come
from a smoke machine, having exactly the intended effect.

When you see a design smell, it's useful to understand it to avoid
growing problems in the future. It might be the source of **accumulating
design debt**: borrowing against the future to quickly solve a problem now.
For example, rolling out a new look and feel to key parts of a product to get
it in the hands of users faster, with the intention to finish cleaning up the
stragglers later. After a dozen such short-term decisions, the product could
start to look like a Frankenstein monster. The problem here is that the

longer it takes to start paying off design debt, the more costly and difficult it is to handle. This risk of design debt needs to be balanced against the need to iteratively deliver value to users. Design smells can help you identify when you're starting to take on too much design debt.

Too Much Information (TMI)

This design smell is noticeable when content is bursting at the seams, such as a listing containing 500 items and no method for users to find relevant items within the list. Unsorted, unchunked, unrelated items bundled together in something generic like "Settings" and no way for users to find the setting they want when they need it. In these cases we can refer back to our patterns from Chapter 3 for finding, reading, collecting, and sharing content, like autocomplete, pagination, filtering, and autocomplete. For an example of Too Much Information, Figure 5-5 shows multiple, scrollable pages of settings in Chrome Dev Tools.

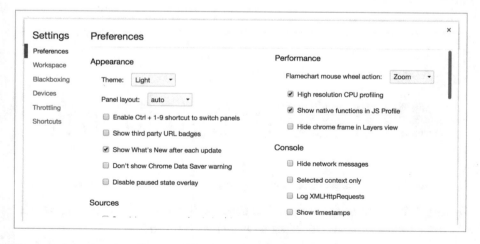

Figure 5-5. *Screenshot of Chrome's Developer Tools with an extraordinary number of settings for their power users*

Given this huge number of settings, the folks at Google introduced a searchable command menu[9] that can be opened from any tab in the developer tools using Cmd+Shift+P (or Ctrl+Shift+P) to autocomplete tools, including settings, as shown in Figure 5-6.

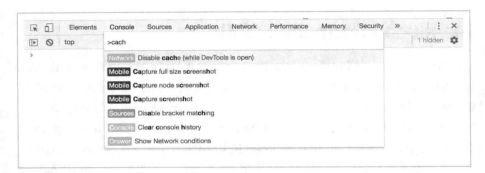

Figure 5-6. *Screenshot of autocomplete dev tools*

Another sign of TMI is the pagination pattern being stretched, as shown in Figure 5-7.

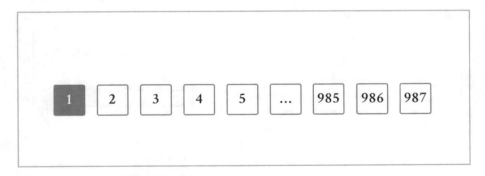

Figure 5-7. *Screenshot of pagination with hundreds and thousands of pages probably doesn't lead to relevant content*

---

[9]Paul Bakaus, "DevTools Digest: More Power with the New Command Menu," https://developers.google.com/web/updates/2016/04/devtools-digest-command-menu, April 2016.

If the number of pages gets too high, this is a design smell that further refinement is needed through, for example, search filtering. Meanwhile, Google's approach to the decreasing relevance of search results is a design that suggests that there are only ever 10 pages, as shown in Figure 5-8.

Figure 5-8. *Screenshot of Google's pagination only shows 10 pages*

The reality is that navigating to page 10 reveals that there actually are more pages, as shown in Figure 5-9.

Figure 5-9. *Screenshot of Google's pagination has more than 10 pages*

Modals and pop-ups

Modal UI pattern

A **modal** (or "modal window," "dialog," "overlay," or "lightbox," sometimes described as a "pop-up") is an overlay that places the system in another mode, temporarily displaying different content.

Figure 5-10 shows an example of a modal.

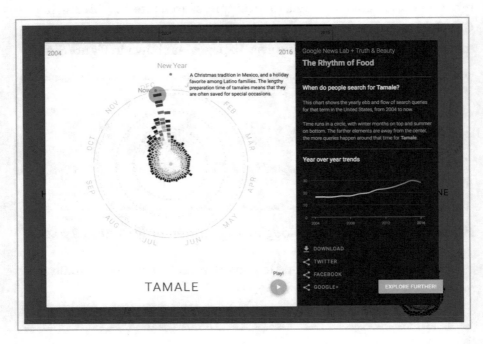

Figure 5-10. *Screenshot of Google's lightbox content modal that tells you more about specific items*

Modals contain smaller pieces of new content, while the rest of the screen is covered with a transparent overlay. When using a modal, provide an exit mechanism like closing × symbols, "Close" links, or clicking the transparent overlay. Figure 5-11 shows an example of a closing × symbol to dismiss the modal.

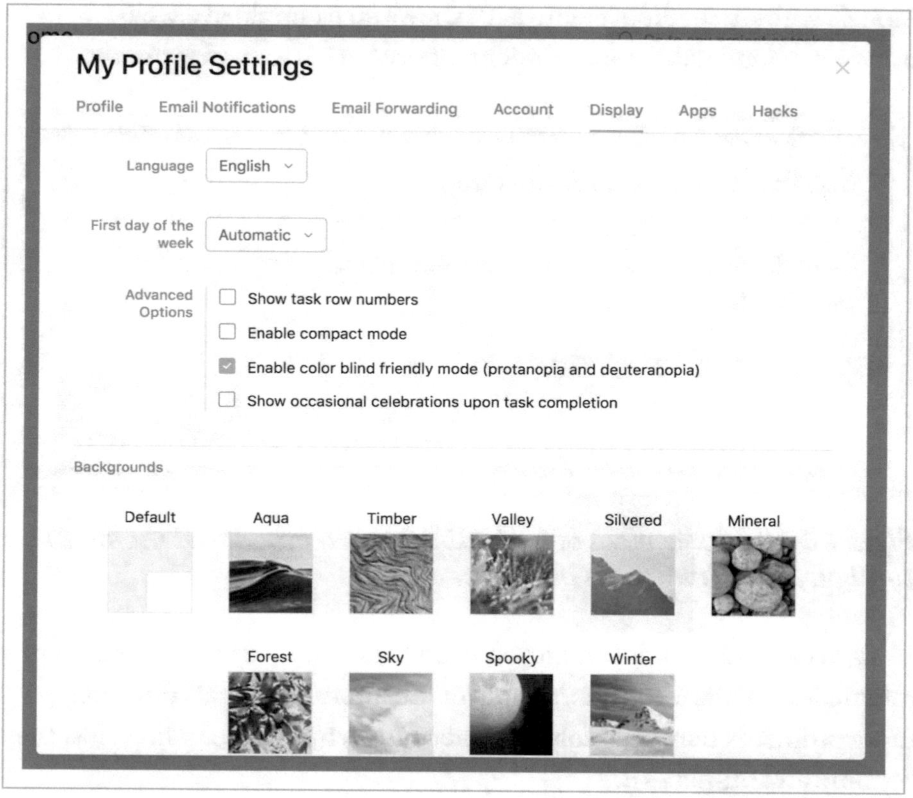

My Profile Settings

Profile   Email Notifications   Email Forwarding   Account   Display   Apps   Hacks

Language   English ∨

First day of the week   Automatic ∨

Advanced Options   ☐ Show task row numbers
☐ Enable compact mode
☑ Enable color blind friendly mode (protanopia and deuteranopia)
☐ Show occasional celebrations upon task completion

Backgrounds

Default   Aqua   Timber   Valley   Silvered   Mineral

Forest   Sky   Spooky   Winter

Figure 5-11. *Screenshot of a property modal to edit profile settings in Asana*

If there is a destructive action in the modal (e.g., it's a confirmation modal for deleting content) and the destructive action cannot be undone easily, it is safer to make the default "Enter" key action a cancellation option.

For titles and buttons, a brief verb and noun pair like "Create project" or "Send invitation" clarifies the reason for the interruption from regular content and what you're expected to do next. For a person to efficiently navigate your modal, they can almost make a decision about what to do by reading *only* the button—helpful for people that compulsively dismiss modals without reading. Figure 5-12 shows an example of a well-labeled button in a modal that people might otherwise fail to read properly.

Figure 5-12. *Screenshot of LinkedIn shows a functional modal to configure your invitation before sending it*

You can use a modal when you need to change the flow of content or interaction. While a common staple of the Internet, modals often cause more problems than they solve and need to be handled carefully, lest they become an anti-pattern.

Figure 5-13 shows an unprompted bulletin modal changing the flow of content or interaction from the activity the user was performing.

Figure 5-13. *Screenshot of Asana's bulletin modal advertising a new feature in a premium product*

Modal design smell

The primary purpose of a modal—disrupting the flow to temporarily change mode—suggests that there's a deeper root cause underlying what's wrong with the UI. Why would you need to disrupt the flow? The existing flow must be somehow insufficient to the task at hand. It is, however, only a smell; a modal might be the best option for the context.

Pop-up anti-pattern

Modals are occasionally referred to as pop-ups. The original "pop-ups," however, used specific browser behavior to intrusively pop up without any warning and are typically blocked in modern browsers. As an exaggerated, evil-twin anti-pattern name for modals though, "pop-ups" is suitable enough: they often pop up to a user's great annoyance.

The problem the pop-up is trying to solve is how to draw a user's attention to a Call To Action. This happens a lot on web sites with a strong content marketing focus. That is, they draw people in with their "free" content, then "ask" for something else, like a newsletter subscription to generate leads or signup to a subscription service for monthly sales. As such, including this Call To Action beside or after the content might not give it enough attention.

The symptoms of a misused modal pop-up are as follows:

- Unless particular care is taken and testing performed, pop-ups are frequently highly confusing and **difficult to operate** for people using keyboards, screen readers, or assistive devices.

- On smaller screens such as a mobile phone, pop-ups disrupt the flow completely by **covering the entire screen**. In this case, it would make more sense to defer the content to a subsequent page. If there is so little content in the pop-up that it has room to spare, then a pop-up is overkill and might be replaced with inline content (under a collapsible, disclosure element, for example).

- When system-generated rather than user-initiated, pop-ups are **highly disruptive, working against user expectations**. Some folk use proxies for determining the user's intent like moving the mouse cursor to the close tab button to indicate intention to leave. When the "intent" is not captured properly, the disruptive effect of the intrusion is aggravated. For example, scrolling down is no guarantee that a user has read the article and now wants to share it. Finally, these pop-ups obscure the content the user actually intended to read.

- Thanks to habituation, many people **dismiss pop-ups instinctively** without considering their content.

- **Scrollable pop-ups are difficult to navigate**. For example, on a mobile device if a pop-up has a large margin around it, there might be only a small touchable area for scrolling. To scroll within the pop-up, the user might accidentally dismiss it or click a button inside it.

- **Zooming in on images** in lightbox pop-ups can do weird, unexpected things, distorting the UI and obscuring the image.

- **"Mode errors"** occur when the user is not in the mode they expect, leading them to go down the wrong path. For example, you're typing away writing your password into a login form when a newsletter signup form appears, causing you to type your password into that field instead.

- **Cascading pop-ups**—one over the top of the other—disrupt the user even further from their original task, clutter the interface, and are difficult to manage.

Figure 5-14 shows an example of cascading pop-ups.

Figure 5-14. *Screenshot of Asana's cascading pop-ups, leading away from the main page*

There are several alternatives you can use to replace modal pop-ups completely:

- Immediately present actions inline (e.g., display a button group instead of a modal with options).

- Display content inline (e.g., expand a collapsible "disclosure" element to house the new content).

- Defer the content completely to another page.

- Use tooltips (that respond to positioning near screen edges, otherwise you'll still have issues on tiny screens).

- Use one of the notifications we saw in Chapter 2, like the snackbars, toasts, or page-wide fixed notification bars.

Short of that, what steps can you take to minimize the impact of the annoying modal pop-up?

- Always avoid stealing focus. If a user is typing elsewhere, they probably don't mean to be typing in your pop-up.

- Let the user initiate the modal on demand (practicing progressive disclosure).

- Provide easy exits like hitting the escape key, clicking on the overlay, and a well-labeled "Close" link.

- Make it accessible. At a minimum, you probably want `role="dialog"`, `aria-labelledby`, and `aria-describedby` attributes, as well as using JavaScript to move focus to the modal when the user triggers it and restore focus after it's dismissed.[10]

- Ensure relevant content is still in view.

Figure 5-15 shows an example of a modal with a tab bar and internal scrolling. It's possible this much content would be better served in its own space, keeping all of the relevant content in view at once.

---

[10]Learn more about accessible modal dialogs from Marco's Accessibility Blog (`www.marcozehe.de/2015/02/05/advanced-aria-tip-2-accessible-modal-dialogs/`).

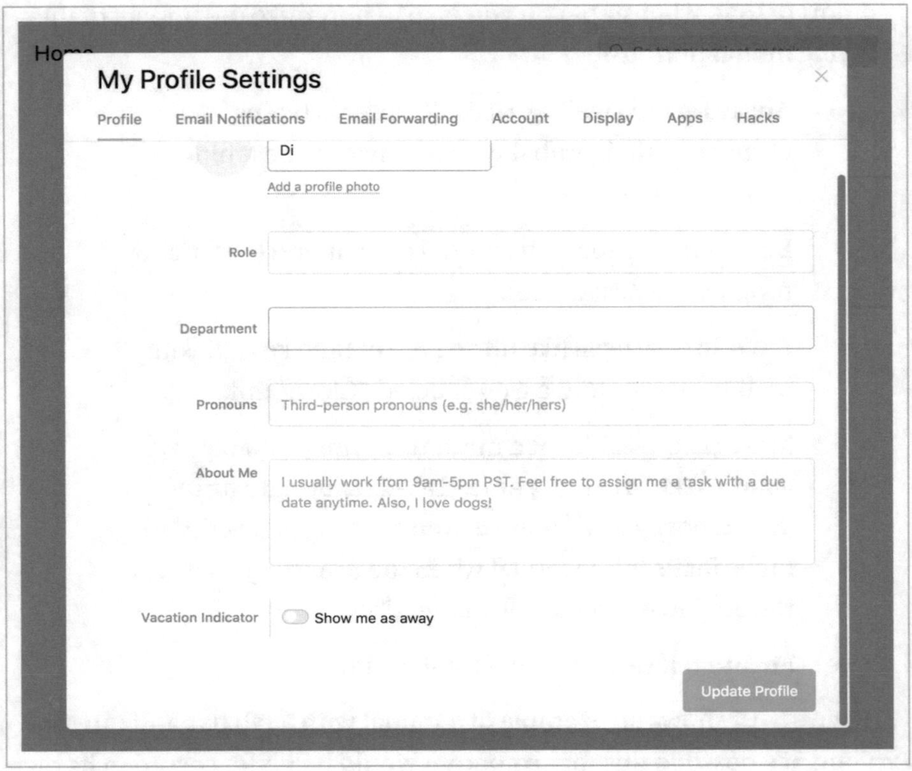

Figure 5-15. *Screenshot of Asana using a scrollable modal*

Note   Tab closed; didn't read (`http://tabcloseddidntread.com/`) is a gallery site calling out organizations that obscure content and provides browser extensions to people to streamline the process of tweeting at organizations to express discontent. This says something about how much frustration pop-ups can cause to some people.

"Overall pattern" design smell

When creating or documenting patterns in a design system, if you see an overall pattern or a "parent pattern," that's a design smell. Using our modal pattern as an example, modals are sometimes categorized into different types, such as "property, function, process, and bulletin" dialog boxes as described in About Face by Alan Cooper.[11] These can be useful and meaningful distinctions. As they appear in a design system, however, this categorization might not be meaningful to an engineer implementing them if they're all styled the same and have the same interactions and behaviors. Bundling different patterns under one overall pattern is a smell.

In the world of software patterns, Martin Fowler suggests "that you often have choices between turning two related concepts into separate patterns, or combining them as variations of a single pattern" and that "if you do split them, don't try to have an overall pattern too." While this risks some duplicated documentation across each variant, you avoid the challenges of an overall pattern being stretched ineffectively to serve too many purposes.[12]

You might be better off splitting similar concepts into named variants like a "benefits modal"[13] without a mutual parent. If that doesn't make sense for your situation, the other possible problem from this design smell is that the variations are too small and not meaningful, which suggests that you have an undesirable inconsistency in your product. Instead of a parent "modal" pattern and a few children variation modal patterns, you might need to consolidate the differences into one modal, producing a more consistent and predictable experience for end users as well as designers

---

[11]Alan Cooper, "About Face," http://shop.oreilly.com/product/9781118766576.do.

[12]Martin Fowler, "Writing Software Patterns," www.martinfowler.com/articles/writingPatterns.html.

[13]Atlassian Design, "Benefits modal" https://atlassian.design/guidelines/product/patterns/user-value-modals.

and developers navigating your design system. Alternatively, what you might be looking at is actually different options and states for a single modal. One modal pattern might be executed in a component with options for positive information styling vs. warning styling for destructive actions, but the pattern stays the same.

The lifetime of a bad pattern

While anti-patterns and dark patterns tend to prioritize short-term gain or superficial wins, within a few years it becomes evident to both consumers and the design community that a pattern is not worth it and it falls out of fashion. Consumers become savvier about the negative impact dark patterns have on them and revolt. They vote with their dollars by switching to products that are easier to use and more trustworthy, so businesses scramble to adapt and strive for creating positive user experiences as a competitive advantage. Designers start to see the long-term costs of the seemingly useful solutions, and so stop using these patterns in new projects. UI design patterns usually have a clear visual component to help people recognize them and have measurable impact on usability in UX metrics like engagement that give visibility to the drawbacks of anti-patterns over time.

As each new dark pattern arises, governments start to ban them, corporations start to penalize them, and legal action can be brought against them. For example, an EU consumer directive outlaws "Sneak into Basket" opt-out add-on purchases, among other dark patterns.[14] Similarly,

---

[14]90 Percent of Everything, "Some Dark Patterns now illegal in UK – interview with Heather Burns," www.90percentofeverything.com/2014/08/26/some-dark-patterns-now-illegal-in-uk-interview-with-heather-burns/.

Google penalizes intrusive interstitial ads[15] and LinkedIn settled a $13M class-action law suit for spamming friends of users.[16]

In the future, we'll see fewer and fewer!

---

[15]Jacob Kastrenakes, "Google will punish sites that use annoying pop-up ads," www. theverge.com/2016/8/23/12610890/google-search-punish-pop-ups-interstitial-ads.

[16]John Brownlee, "After Lawsuit Settlement, LinkedIn's Dishonest Design Is Now A $13 Million Problem," www.fastcompany.com/3051906/after-lawsuit-settlement-linkedins-dishonest-design-is-now-a-13-million-problem.

CHAPTER 6

Mixing and matching patterns

If you have literally tried every possible variation, you will have come across the best solution.

—Julie Zhuo

Now it's time to weave together patterns into a cohesive whole. We have individual UI patterns under our belt, knowledge of how to learn more, and knowledge of how to develop a design system. We know what anti-patterns and dark patterns look like, so we can avoid them. In this chapter, we'll bring together everything we've learned so far, check out how to mix and match patterns effectively, and explore when and how to break away from patterns. We'll concentrate on the familiar and practical domain of e-commerce.

To begin, we'll explore a common feature of e-commerce products: scoped searches.

© Diana MacDonald 2019
D. MacDonald, *Practical UI Patterns for Design Systems*,
https://doi.org/10.1007/978-1-4842-4938-3_6

How to combine patterns successfully to build a more complex UI: Scoped searches example

I'm going to share with you eight approaches to combining patterns successfully to build complex user interfaces.

In previous chapters, we explored search filters, autocomplete, pagination, infinite scroll, and thumbnail patterns. We're now going to see how to combine these concepts into one feature: scoped search.

Scoped search isn't exactly a pattern, as the context and details of the solution are completely different rather than recurring. The only recurring part is the problem. The majority of e-commerce stores share a common usability challenge: how to help shoppers swiftly find products they want to buy. Within a large product range of hundreds or thousands of items, the number of choices to be made can be paralyzing, and the task of navigating them can be overwhelming. In many cases, you'll find categories of products that trim down the total possible search space of items by removing entire groups of products. Instead of searching all of Amazon, for example, you might explore just "horror" movies. This is the idea behind scoped searches.

We'll explore a few variations on how scoped search can appear and function. This will demonstrate how patterns vary in the wild and how combining them in different ways can produce different results and give you ideas around the kinds of forces that influence the appropriateness of each approach.

Reuse elements across patterns: Categories as search filters

Initially, let's consider one particular kind of filter: categories. As an example, Nordstrom lets shoppers navigate directly to categories and subcategories   of content via their dropdown mega menu, shown in Figure 6-1.

Figure 6-1. *Screenshot of Nordstorm's mega menu*

Each category and subcategory is a link.

In Figure 6-2, you can see that when the shopper has navigated specifically to "Pumps," that text is shown in the breadcrumb trail in the top–left of the page.

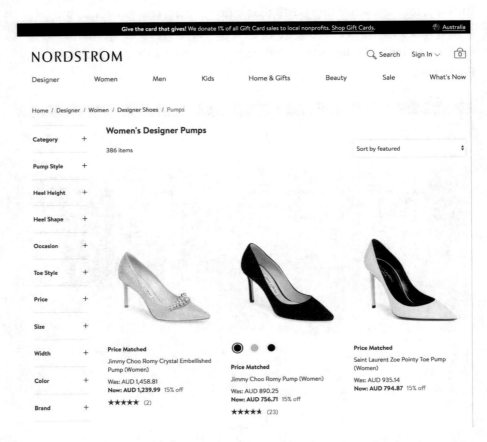

Figure 6-2. *Screenshot of Nordstrom's breadcrumb trail showing the hierarchy of this subcategory*

These categories group content together in a useful manner and let shoppers navigate through a hierarchical structure to find the collection of products of most interest to them. In addition to drilling down through the hierarchy of categories and subcategories, each category is accessible within the filter menu itself as a search filter dimension, as shown in Figure 6-3.

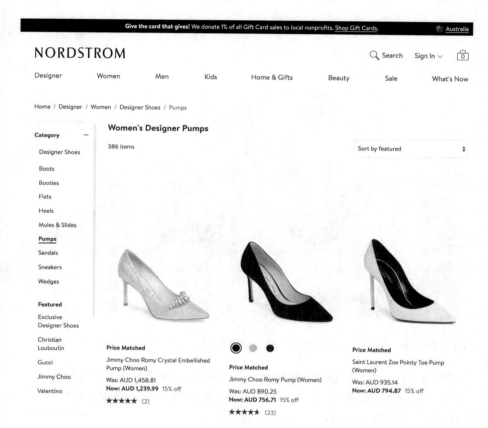

Figure 6-3. *Screenshot of "Pumps" in the breadcrumb trail as well as the selected filter dimension*

Within categories, Nordstrom provide category-specific filters, such as "Pump Style." In Figure 6-4, you can see the "Kitten Heel" filter is selected for the "Pump Style" filter dimension.

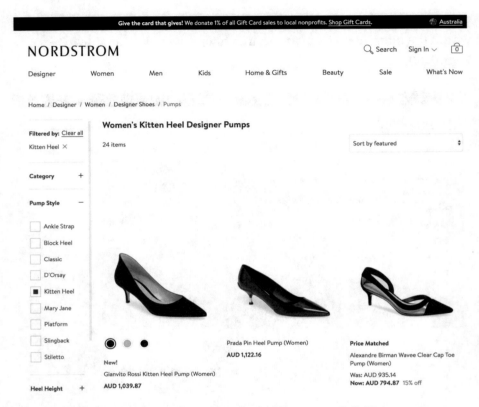

Figure 6-4. *Screenshot of Nordstrom's "Pump Style" filter options*

These category-specific filters are unavailable from other, higher-level categories. In Figure 6-5, you can see there's a "Heel Height" filter dimension for "Women's Designer Shoes."

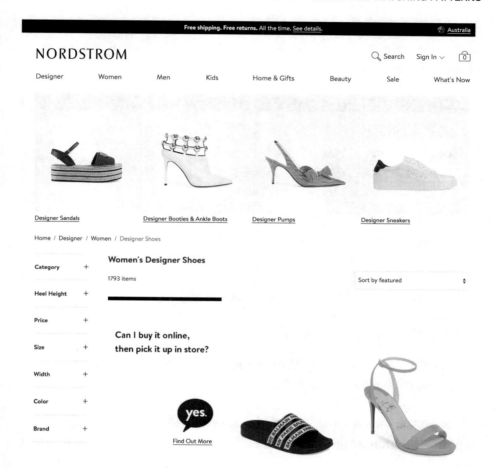

Figure 6-5. *Screenshot of "Women's Designer Shoes" without a "Pump Style" filter*

While in the "Women's Designer Shoes" category, there's no "Pump Style" filter dimension, which is specific to the "Pumps" subcategory.

While categories and filters are usually two sides of the same coin, the ability to have category-specific filters provides a useful distinction between what should be a visually prioritized category filter and what should be a regular search filter. That is, if a group of products can have its own special filters that don't apply to other groups of products, it can be a category.

Nordstrom also let shoppers search for products using an autosuggest form of autocomplete that specifies the category of different results, as shown in Figure 6-6.

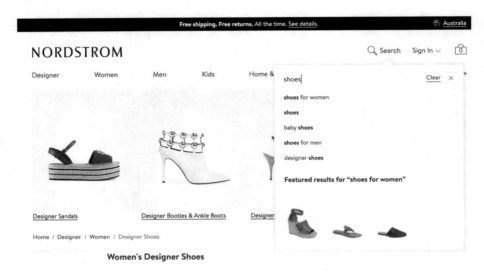

Figure 6-6. *Screenshot of Nordstrom's autosuggest categories, subcategories, and featured results*

Here, the search term "shoes" shows results for different groups of products including "shoes for women" and "shoes for men" as well as just "shoes."

In this Nordstrom example of scoped search, you can see elements reused across patterns. Categories are used as regular hierarchical categories to browse content as well as search filters. Nordstrom uses subcategories as search filters of categories. The "Pumps" category element is used as the category for browsing and a search filter for filtering the "Designer Shoes" category.

In Chapter 3, we studied the search filter pattern's context, problem, and solution. The shopper problem in the Nordstrom example fits the search filter pattern problem: there are lots of items, and the shopper needs to reduce them so they can find the product that fits their criteria. It also fits the context of when to use this solution: there are thousands of items, and filter facets are straightforward.

Cut duplicate content from combined patterns: Categories as search terms

Pinterest treats search terms as categories, offering more categories as you drill down. In Figure 6-7, you can see the search term "wine rack" shows suggested categories, such as "Under Stairs."

Figure 6-7. *Screenshot of Pinterest's category suggestions*

Figure 6-8 shows what happens when you select the "Under Stairs" category: the text is added to your previous search query.

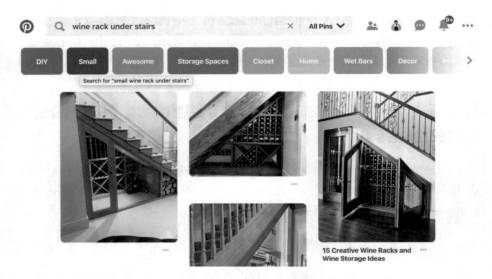

Figure 6-8. *Screenshot of Pinterest's amended search query*

This reinforces the relationship between search and categories in Pinterest's world.

As you hover over a category, you see a tooltip, "Search for "small wine rack under stairs"." Without this additional clue, sighted users might infer the relationship between the search term and the category by their visual proximity and prior familiarity with the search filters pattern. With the tooltip, however, sighted users can confirm that selecting this category is drilling deeper into the "wine rack" journey, instead of leaving wine rack for a new "Under Stairs" search. This text may be even more useful to visually impaired people navigating the page using a screen reader, potentially lacking the visual information to otherwise infer the behavior. This text might even be useful to alternative "user agents," such as search engine bots to make sense of the page.

Elsewhere in the wild, you might find something similar to this but with more repetition. Pinterest could, for example, have included the text "Search results for wine rack" under the categories. They could have shown "wine rack DIY," "wine rack ideas," and so on, repeating "wine rack" in every option. They could have shown "Search for "wine rack"" and the category name for every category. They could have shown "wine rack >" in a breadcrumb trail. Instead, Pinterest's approach to combining patterns is minimalist, cutting any potential duplicate content.

In the Pinterest example of scoped search, duplicate content is cut instead of repeating shared element across patterns. This makes sense for their business's context. As a visual discovery tool that focuses on content[1] and inclusive design,[2] this minimal and accessible approach to scoped search is predictable for their product. In the Nordstrom example, we saw more repeated text in details such as the breadcrumb trails than in the Pinterest example. Pinterest's approach suits its visual nature and endless discovery.

Efficiently combine patterns to avoid the need for others: Autosuggest and thumbnails

Similar to the Nordstrom example, Zomato autosuggests results from different categories before visitors type in any search queries, as you can see in Figure 6-9.

---

[1]Andreas Pihlström, "Redesigning Pinterest, block by block," `https://medium.com/@suprb/redesigning-pinterest-block-by-block-6040a00d80a3`, July 2016.

[2]Long Cheng, Pinterest Engineering, "Seven best practices for inclusive product design," `https://medium.com/@Pinterest_Engineering/seven-best-practices-for-inclusive-product-design-9476c61f1e17`, April 2018.

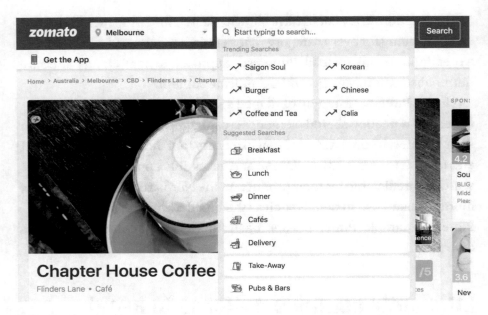

Figure 6-9. *Screenshot of Zomato autosuggesting trending searches and meal time categories before you search for anything*

After starting to type in a search query, Zomato autosuggests results from various categories, including a suburb, a "Collection," a "Cuisine," and a "Dish," as shown in Figure 6-10.

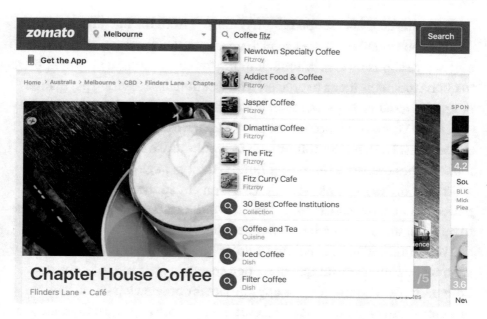

Figure 6-10. *Screenshot of Zomato's autosuggest results from a variety of categories*

In that example, the results that show a photo link to specific results whereas the results with a search icon link to a search results page with more filtering options.

In contrast to Nordstrom, Zomato helps visitors visualize different categories and results using thumbnails (illustrations, photographs, and icons) to preview upcoming results. If there were no thumbnails, it might be harder for people to visualize the content and understand what each means. To discover what they mean, the user might need to go through a process of trial and error to test each one and see if it matches their desires or not. In that scenario, each time the user returned to the search, they'd need a method for restoring their previous search text and a way of knowing which items they'd tried already. That might lead to a "recent searches" feature or "visited links" styling. Using thumbnails could mean you don't need to build these other elements.

This search is also scoped to "Melbourne" from the location category.

The thumbnails here are useful to preview a small number of items (up to ten) before choosing one. Without limiting the suggestions to ten items, there might be too many items to preview with thumbnails, requiring pagination or infinite scrolling in the autocomplete, which could be awkward.

In the Zomato example of scoped search, we see that thumbnails in autosuggest (rather than thumbnails in results as we saw with Pinterest) make it unnecessary to employ infinite scrolling, pagination, "recent searches," or "visited link" styling. This is an efficient combination of patterns that achieves user goals while avoiding alternative technical work to build features that achieve fewer benefits.

We examined thumbnails in Chapter 1 and autocomplete in Chapter 3. Zomato's example of scoped search aligns with the context of both patterns. Thumbnails are appropriate for previewing visual content in a collection of linked resources. Autocomplete is appropriate when you can quickly present matching results from a larger data set using common search terms that fit the search context. Together, they solve the problem of scoping searches.

Zomato's approach of using thumbnails in autocomplete wouldn't make as much sense for Pinterest. A single concept like "wine rack under stairs" could have thousands of visual representations. Using a single thumbnail to preview what will be found in that category's level of detail might be misleading.

Interstitial patterns: Autosuggest and navigable categories

In addition to autosuggest with thumbnails, you might consider navigable categories with thumbnails.

RS is a distributor of electronics, electromechanical, and industrial components. Components companies often exhibit excellent search filtering behavior because their shoppers often need precise results—highly specified products where no substitute will do. Here, you can see a search for "Cherry switch" on RS's Australian web site first suggests that you choose a category for the results that can quickly remove irrelevant results, as shown in Figure 6-11.

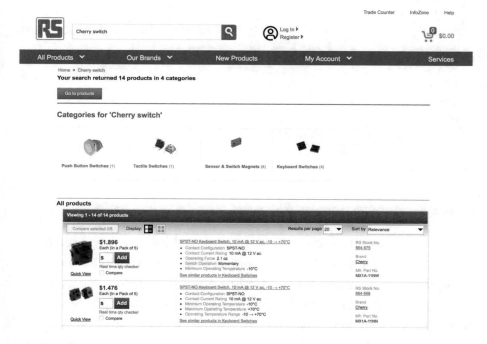

Figure 6-11. *Screenshot of RS search results includes available categories for the searched term as well as a result listing*

Using a category selection, a shopper can narrow the results from 14 down to 4 by selecting "Keyboard Switches" as the category of interest, as shown in Figure 6-12.

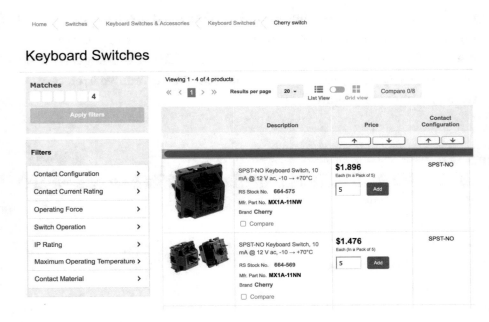

Figure 6-12. Screenshot of RS's categorized search results

This is important when an e-commerce store has a highly diverse product range, because there's a higher chance of overlap in terms used in multiple categories that are completely irrelevant to others. The shopper may not think of their desired product as a "Sensor & Switch Magnet," but indicating the different categories using imagery lets shoppers quickly identify the one that's relevant to them through immediate recognition and ignore the other categories. If this category selection wasn't available, they may not recognize irrelevant results as quickly in the table listing itself when they're all jumbled up together, leaving them to wade through more noise.

From the category, the shopper can see clearly by the H1 page title that they are within the "Keyboard Switches" category now rather than the search page they were previously. The search term is still applicable though as evidenced by: the results themselves as well as "Cherry switch" shown in the breadcrumbs trail (after the "Keyboard Switches" category and within "Switches" and "Keyboard Switches & Accessories"). Now the shopper can further filter the available results to only switches with an operating force of "45N," as shown in Figure 6-13.

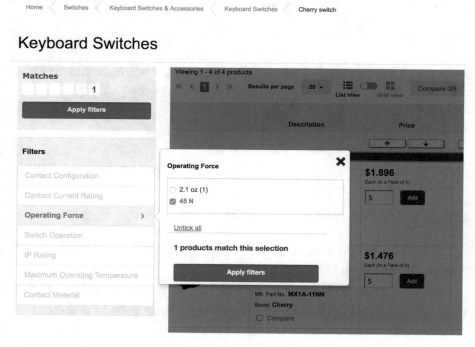

Figure 6-13. *Screenshot of RS's filtering options for categorized search results*

After filtering, the shopper can see that there is one match from filtering, that filters are applied, that the "Operating Force" filter dimension is applied, and that the filter dimension is filtered to results with a value of "45 N," as shown in Figure 6-14.

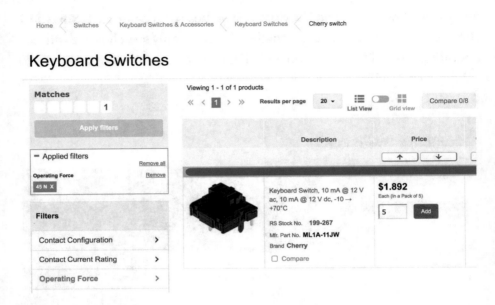

Figure 6-14. *Screenshot of RS's filtered results*

The shopper can then remove one filter at a time or all of them at once (which in this case has the same result).

Alternatively, the shopper could visit the "Keyboard Switches" category itself, as shown in Figure 6-15, without filtering the results by a search.

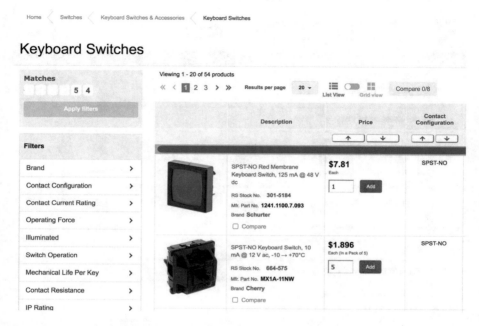

Figure 6-15. *Screenshot of RS's category browsing*

This lets shoppers discover other content within the same section starting with something they know.

As another option, the shopper could use the available autosuggest search to navigate directly to the "Cherry" brand index page, as shown in Figure 6-16.

Figure 6-16. *Screenshot of RS's brand index page*

As you can see, categories, filters, and searches each refine the total available results by the shopper's needs using different methods. They can complement each other or be used independently to navigate content via different paths.

In the RS example of scoped search, there is a step in between the search and showing the full results listing—to present thumbnails for categories. These categories further scoped the search results using the thumbnail pattern. The shopper can then further refine results using standard search filters without thumbnails. This interstitial use of thumbnail categories might be used only when the primary path would lead to too many search results or mixed results that are difficult to understand.

The use of interstitial thumbnails for categories here fits the context of RS's customer base and extensive product range. If a Nordstrom shopper searched for "shoes" and selected "shoes" instead of "shoes for men," they'd still be in a good position to apply the "Men's Shoes" search filter afterward and know what to expect about the appearance of men's shoes. There's less risk that they won't understand what the other items are when they see women's shoes in the results. They might intentionally want to see men's and women's shoes together and use other filters like price and color to reduce results. RS's visual categories can help explain results and remove irrelevant ones. An intervening step like RS's to show category thumbnails on Nordstrom's site may just distract from the results without adding clarity.

Visually combine and distinguish patterns: Categories in tabbed navigation

A popular remix of search filters and categories includes tabbed navigation.

When combining search and categories, it's useful to lean on classic design principles such as hierarchy and unity to demonstrate the relationship between the search terms and categories. For example, Google's Search product lets you search for a term, such as "Melbourne," and see "All" results, as shown in the tab navigation bar, as shown in Figure 6-17.

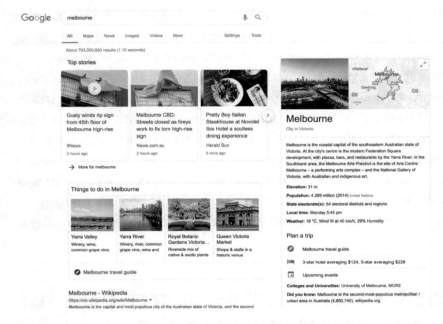

Figure 6-17. *Screenshot of Google's "All" results search scope*

Here, Google shows a mix of content types, highlighting what might be the most relevant content across sections.

After this, you can then limit your results to a single category using the tab navigation, as shown in Figure 6-18.

Figure 6-18. *Screenshot of Google's "Videos" search scope*

If you're logged in, you can further tailor your results using an additional "Personal" category, which includes information from Gmail, as shown in Figure 6-19.

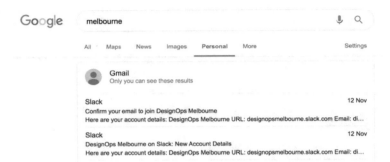

Figure 6-19. *Screenshot of Google's "Personal" search scope*

By showing the search input first, followed by the categories in the tab navigation underneath, Google reveals that the tab navigation groups content *within* the search. This works really well because Google provides sufficient content within each category that a visitor will rarely find a tab without any results (more likely millions of results).

Let's consider another example. Coles supermarket chain shows the search input and additional tabbed navigation in the same logical order as Google's search and categories. In Figure 6-20, you can see a specific, selected category (a list of favorites).

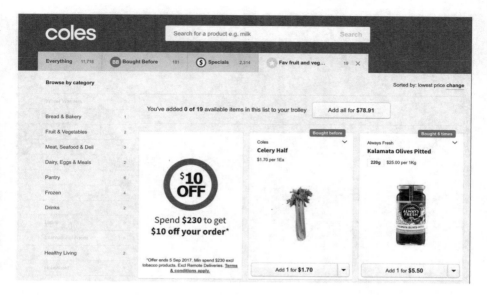

Figure 6-20. *Screenshot of Coles "Fav fruit and vegetables" list category*

Note   Coles shows the number of results contained within each category and within each filter and disables all filters with 0 results.

In this instance, the shopper has navigated directly to this category. When the shopper then performs their first search for something that happens to be excluded from the filtered category, they find disappointing results, as shown in Figure 6-21.

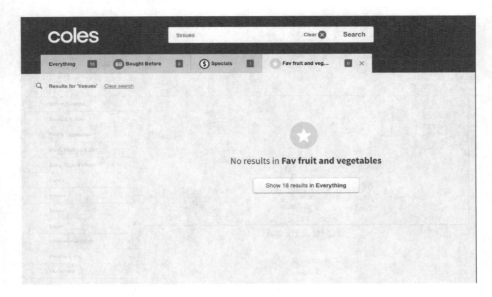

Figure 6-21. *Screenshot of Coles "Fav fruit and vegetables" when searching for "tissues"*

Because the shopper has used the filters as navigation first (instead of search before filters), they might be disoriented by the lack of results without recognizing that the new search did not clear the selected category filter. Imagine instead that the categories tab navigation appeared *before* the search input: it would then appear that the category was being filtered by the search results (rather than the search filtered by categories), more closely matching the shopper's mental model formed by their user journey. As such, they might realize before searching for "tissues" that they'll need to navigate out of this category.

In this scenario, Coles helpfully provides a Call To Action button on this category's zero results screen to inspire shoppers to expand their search results by leaving this category and filtering instead by the "Everything" category, which shows all results for the "tissues" search. This is a good default to use instead of a blank slate, helping visitors recover from dead ends. Alternatively, to avoid zero results screens, you might suggest alternate words or spellings.

The tabbed navigation and scoped search examples illustrate two particular considerations to the category approach. One is that you can provide a smoother experience with fewer points of friction by avoiding zero results screens if search results can be found for all category filters. Secondly, depending on the path your user has taken, the relationship between search and category filters can be confusing. We'll see more on establishing these relationships in a Flickr example in the section ahead.

In the Google search and Coles shopping examples of scoped search, we see how tabs can be used to indicate categories and filters used to refine searches. The intersection of these two elements can lead to confusion if they're not visually distinguished with paths provided out of each.

Even though these companies are of quite a different scale, there is enough similarity in the context of their visitors' and shoppers' needs that a scoped search using tabbed navigation makes sense for both. The execution of each approach, however, changes to suit their business.

Preserve or discard data in repeated use of patterns: Clearing filters on new searches

When using these extra search filters and related features, you might consider the effect of clearing filters. Again, leaning on classic UI design principles, it's often useful to preserve user's data from previous interactions, but it's necessary to balance that against the risk of dead ends produced by scoped searches.

On Harvard Business Review's (HBR) web site, if you search for "Design systems," you can then apply a filter for "Innovation" to reduce results, as shown in Figure 6-22.

Figure 6-22. *Screenshot of HBR search for "Design systems" filtered by "Innovation" showing 3,026 results*

If you then search for "Design products," the search results listing clears the previous filters for the new search, as shown in Figure 6-23.

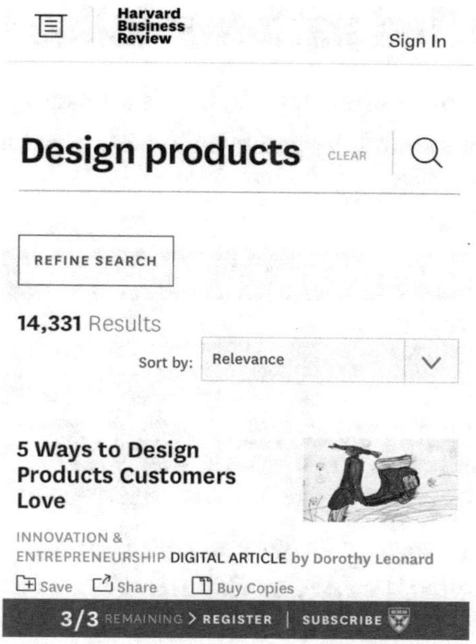

Figure 6-23. *Screenshot of HBR search for "Design products" without "Innovation" filter showing 14,331 results*

Unlike the Coles example, HBR opts to make every search a new search, clearing previous filters. This approach reduces the chances of zero results screens and clarifies the relationship between search and filters (where search trumps filters) but runs the risk that with a lot of filters selected, any change to the search query will undo the visitor's hard work refining results.

In the HBR example of scoped search, subsequent uses of the search clear any search filters, starting over. Coles chooses to preserve all filters until the user makes an explicit choice to remove them.

Clarify repeated patterns: Inline tags

For yet another spin on scoped search, here's an example from Flickr. In their UI, Flickr scopes search by category in a tab nav bar, as shown in Figure 6-24.

Figure 6-24. *Screenshot of Flickr's search that lets you scope a search for "airbnb" by Photos, People, or Groups*

Once you've navigated to a "person" page on Flickr, you can use the inline search icon on the page within "Photostream" to limit searches to this person's photostream. By clicking that search icon, the main search bar is focused and an inline "input tag" is used to show the scope, "Airbnb Community | Photos," as shown in Figure 6-25.

Figure 6-25. *Screenshot of Flickr's scoped search with inline input tags*

This way, Flickr can provide just one search bar and yet preserve the in-page selections, such as "Airbnb Community" and "Photostream" in the example shown.

In the Flickr example of scoped search, you can clarify the relationships between patterns and steps in user interactions by repeating information and subtly adding additional cues to educate the user about what happened and how to interact with the pattern's components.

Evaluate resulting trade-offs: Infinite scroll

In Chapter 3, we saw the drawbacks of using an infinite scrolling favorites list in the Twitter example. It can be difficult or impossible to reach the footer on a long infinite scrolling page if it keeps scrolling away from you as new content loads. It can also be difficult to find a specific piece of content in a long page loading one section at a time. One method for mitigating the impact of these challenges can be seen in L.L.Bean's clothing range UI. Without filtering, 24 products are shown at a time in an infinite scrolling results list (loading in more as you approach the footer), as shown in Figure 6-26.

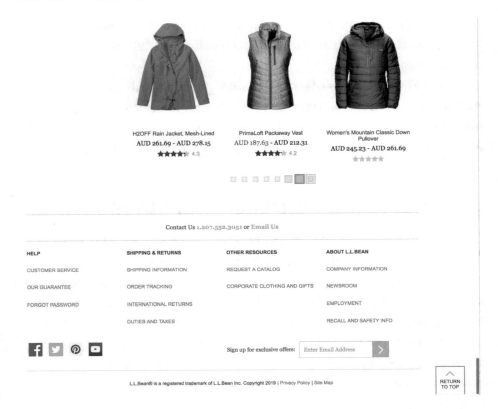

H2OFF Rain Jacket, Mesh-Lined
AUD 261.69 - AUD 278.15
★★★★☆ 4.3

PrimaLoft Packaway Vest
AUD 187.63 - AUD 212.31
★★★★☆ 4.2

Women's Mountain Classic Down Pullover
AUD 245.23 - AUD 261.69
☆☆☆☆☆

Contact Us 1.207.552.3051 or Email Us

HELP

CUSTOMER SERVICE

OUR GUARANTEE

FORGOT PASSWORD

SHIPPING & RETURNS

SHIPPING INFORMATION

ORDER TRACKING

INTERNATIONAL RETURNS

DUTIES AND TAXES

OTHER RESOURCES

REQUEST A CATALOG

CORPORATE CLOTHING AND GIFTS

ABOUT L.L.BEAN

COMPANY INFORMATION

NEWSROOM

EMPLOYMENT

RECALL AND SAFETY INFO

Sign up for exclusive offers: Enter Email Address

L.L.Bean® is a registered trademark of L.L.Bean Inc. Copyright 2019 | Privacy Policy | Site Map

RETURN TO TOP

Figure 6-26. *Screenshot of L.L.Bean infinite scroll starting to load more content*

However, most categories have fewer than 100 products, limiting the number of times a shopper waits for the lazy loaded content to 4 times. In addition, the web site clearly prioritizes search and filtering features, and applying just one filter is enough to reduce the list to a manageable amount of content that infinite scrolling is no longer required, as shown in Figure 6-27.

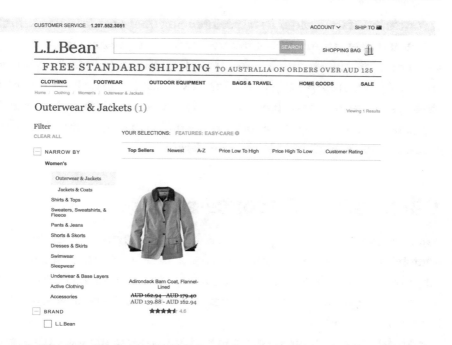

Figure 6-27. *Screenshot of L.L.Bean where one filter reduces the list of results dramatically*

By contrast, if L.L.Bean shoppers instead typically paged through dozens of infinite scrolling sections of results, the balance of filtering and scrolling might be off, suggesting the filters weren't effective enough at reducing results.

In the L.L.Bean example of scoped search, we see how the combination of infinite scrolling and search filters is balanced. The content and interaction path means infinite scrolling usually isn't necessary so it isn't shown. It's only brought to light when the primary path has failed to reduce search space enough to make a decision.

Reflecting back on the Twitter example, infinite scrolling for favorites might have a small conflict in certain contexts. If favorites are used to store content for later and infinite scrolling is used to discover endless new content, the combination be a poor fit. This depends on who is using the

255

favorites list. If the Twitter user is referencing their own favorites, search filters and pagination without infinite scrolling might help them find content more quickly, but if a user is exploring someone else's favorites, an infinite list of surprising new items could be ideal. The infinite scrolling feed is also consistent with every other kind of content on Twitter, making it predictable. L.L.Bean's context is quite different from Twitter's, so the trade-offs to evaluate are also quite different.

Other forms of scoped search

We've seen a variety of scoped search approaches here, mixing and matching patterns we've explored in detail in previous chapters. It's important to note how the intersection of patterns in each approach affects the overall experience. As with patterns, the context to each solution is critical to its success.

You'll discover there are myriad variations out in the wild. It's worth keeping an eye out and noticing when you see a different take on a pattern and try to understand the reasons behind an unusual remix. Often, you'll find there's something particular about the brand, content, constraints, or user context that compels a new design.

Favoriting becomes wish listing

In Chapter 3 we saw how to use favorites to help users track specific, excellent content. Now we'll look at a specific variant of favorites in the world of e-commerce: wish lists. Together, you can drive user behavior and create experiences tailored to your product.

Wish lists/wish listing

A **wish list** is a personalized, curated list of preferred items, stored for later purchase. The subsequent purchase may be made *by* the wish lister or *for* the wish lister by their friends and family.

Figure 6-28 shows an example of wishing listing using a dropdown menu for adding items to a list of your choosing, including a "Wish List."

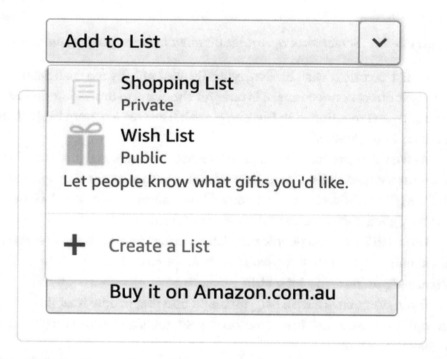

Figure 6-28. *Screenshot of Amazon's Add to List options*

On Amazon, once you've added an item to a wish list, you might "view your list" or "continue shopping." You can also navigate to the wish list via your "Account & Lists" dropdown menu. Figure 6-29 shows the item on the wish list.

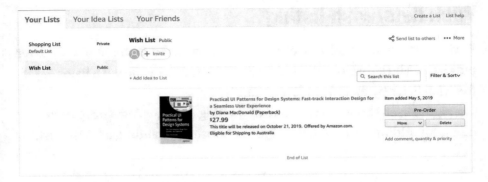

Figure 6-29. *Screenshot of Amazon's wish list containing one item*

Unlike favorites, wish lists are typically used only by the wish lister and their direct connections. It is rarer for shoppers to browse strangers' wish lists. As I mentioned in Chapter 3, wish lists are also more likely than favorites to be private.

As wish lists are sometimes used by a user's friends to figure out what to buy as a gift, wish lists frequently offer alternative purchasing options such as gift cards. You see this in digital book stores such as iBooks where you may gift a book (such as this one!) to a friend.

Use wish lists when people may not make a purchase in the first visit, but keeping track of their top candidates for purchase increases their chance of purchase in a later visit.

If you don't have a wish list, you might find that people treat the shopping cart as a wish list anyway and hold items there until they're ready to make a decision.

Note   An astute reader may notice the "overall pattern" design smell here that we discussed in Chapter 5: Are we treating "favorites" as an "overall pattern" containing "wish lists"? If you're using both wish lists and favorites in your product, you'd do well to clarify their differences and document them separately.

Combining wish listing and lazy signup

In Chapter 2 we investigated the lazy signup pattern. Let's bring that into action with wish listing.

You can offer a wish list without account registration for a single shopping session. Using the wish list, the shopper can gather their top candidates of similar items for purchasing before making a decision on which or how many items they want to buy together. If they cannot make a final decision within a single session, you can provide optional registration to keep the wish list for later using lazy signup.

Figure 6-30 shows an example of a wish list with lazy signup.

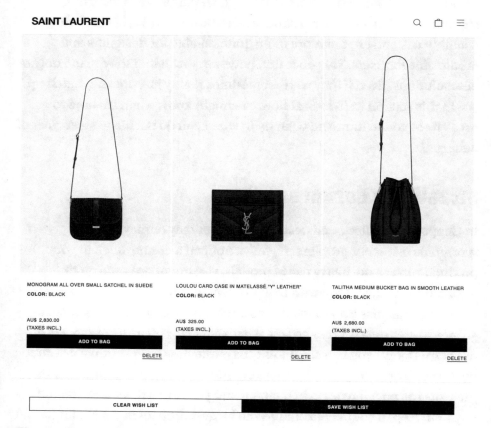

Figure 6-30. *Screenshot of Saint Laurent's wish list*

Here, you can add items to your wish list and view your wish list without creating an account. If you choose "Save wish list," you'll be prompted to log in or register an account.

As you can see, the wish list and lazy signup patterns work seamlessly together without any changes or amendments. This is actually the ninth approach for combining patterns: do nothing special at all.

Next, we'll explore what to do when patterns are the wrong approach.

When and how to break away from patterns

To reiterate our definition from Chapter 1, UI patterns are recurring solutions to UI problems in a context. They are recurring because they usually work and are therefore often quite reliable for designers and predictable for users. This does not, however, mean that they're the only or best solutions. Even if they were, sometimes reality just doesn't match up.

In this section we'll look at how you might know when it's time to break from convention and what to do when you do decide to steer clear of patterns.

Investigate design smells

In Chapter 5, we discussed design smells that may or may not be symptoms of deeper problem. If you've noticed a design smell in your product, such as the heavy use of modals, you might do some quick research to validate if there's a real problem or not.

Using analytics (www.uxbooth.com/articles/complete-beginners-guide-to-web-analytics-and-measurement/) for measuring aspects of user experience, you can see if this area is affecting your product's desired outcomes. For example, if the checkout process of your e-commerce site presents the payment form in a modal and your analytics show that the payment step of your checkout has the biggest drop off in your sales funnel (i.e., it's the biggest contributor to cart abandonment), that suggests your hunch about the modal smell might be right. Then it's time to investigate why that is the case, validating your quantified usability problem with qualitative research to get the information needed to make a decision about it.

You might then perform some usability testing with three diverse representatives from your target audience. Suppose two of your testers sail through the test flawlessly and one stumbles because the payment form shows an alarmingly high shipping fee for their remote location. We can then circle back to our quantitative data to see if this could be the cause of the cart abandonment. Let's imagine this shipping destination accounts for only 0.05% of your site traffic—this couldn't explain the volume of cart abandonment. It's worth considering, but let's also test with two more people.

This time, we find the modal content isn't scaling well and doesn't fit on iPhone screens making it hard to scroll and navigate. This time we see iPhone accounts for 40% of site traffic. Sure enough, when we slice our traffic by device, we see 70% of cart abandonment at the payment step is on iPhone. Now we know it's time to reconsider our modal.

In this way, we've followed the symptoms of a design smell to discover our misused modal has become a popup anti-pattern. Next, we'll consider what to do with our identified problem.

Review pattern principles for identified usability problems

You might reconsider a pattern when you've identified a usability problem in its execution. Once you've identified it, you have a few options for addressing it.

You might be thinking that this usability problem doesn't mean the modal is a poor choice, just that *this* modal is poorly done.

This moment is a useful prompt to reconsider if we've correctly aligned the problem and context with the modal solution. A modal is a disruption to a normal flow. Does is make sense to distract the shopper from the task of purchasing an item in a checkout by a change in flow? Possibly. A Baymard Institute study on checkout usability[3] showed that people had a higher degree of trust in payment forms that were visually distinguished from the rest of the checkout, as if it is a more sensitive task so it needs a more "secure" design (even though that's not really how security works). A modal might be a suitable method for visually distinguishing the payment form. So, updating the modal design and improving the engineering execution might be the best path forward to provide a better experience and improve conversions.

On the other hand, let's revisit our modal pattern's details and what other patterns we could use instead. A payment form rules out using a notification or tooltip. While we could display the form inline, it might be better to defer the payment form to another page, styled to engender trust in its security.

So, what would it take to update our modal's visual style and implementation vs. replacing it with a new page? Are there other benefits to be gained from either approach? If you're undecided, you might test a prototype of each approach before building either. Based on principles alone, you might decide to try the page. In that particular case, you might A/B test the new page on a small subset of your audience before rolling it out to everyone.

Review problem and context

One reason that usability problems might arise using perfectly reasonable patterns is that we sometimes fail to clarify the user problem in the first place.

---

[3]https://baymard.com/blog/perceived-security-of-payment-form.

In Chapter 3 we looked at a few methods for establishing the context in a design problem. Suppose the payment form had failed because it didn't include a gift card redemption option and the true context of the situation was that the shopper was in fact a gift card recipient cashing in their gift from a friend. The challenge is not that your payment form solution was a poor fit for the problem (making a payment) but that the problem (sending money) didn't match the context (redeeming a gift card instead of sending money).

When you've identified a usability problem, you may wish to clarify the context before assuming the solution is a bad fit.

With effective user research and collaboration within your organization, you can accurately identify all relevant aspects of the context that affect decision. These include the user journeys, user tasks, personas, constraints, content, and data we considered in Chapter 3. The very real business and technical constraints of your organization might prevent the use of a particular solution: sometimes reliable infinite scrolling just isn't feasible.

Another scenario to consider which might lead to misaligned context and problem is the "but that's what Google do" situation. You are not Google (https://blog.bradfieldcs.com/you-are-not-google-84912cf44afb). Sometimes a pattern used by a big player in the industry might be relevant to their business in a way that it just can't be to yours. Conversely, just because they're doing it doesn't mean it's the best choice—big companies can be at risk of inertia through bureaucracy, even when they've identified their own usability problems.

Strive for predictability

One of the strengths of using the proven solutions found in patterns is that they are familiar to users and therefore predictable. What happens then when there's tension between external conventions and internal consistency?

Sometimes as designers we need to make a choice between the industry-leading approach and the internally consistent approach, particularly if we have lots of design debt holding us back. If we choose to push one part of a product forward with modern styles and proven patterns, while the rest of the product continues to have awkward, old styles and behaviors, our users might find it even harder to use because it's inconsistent. On the other hand, sticking to weird, old quirks in the UI might be easier for repeat users once they've figured out how it works.

One way to address this problem is to update whole pages and sections of your product at a time with a new look and feel along with the new patterns. Your users might then be able to predict the product's behavior by considering which part they're in. Continuing in this way, you might avoid updating only one component in a page at a time. Leaving one part behaving the old way and another part in a different way could lead to more confusion overall.

Innovate

Sometimes the best path is the road less traveled. When you need your product to stand out in a crowded market, innovating away from the standard solutions to problems might help. In these cases, you can benchmark and user test your alternative solutions.

Back in 2017, before Snapchat's controversial 2018 redesign,[4] it was a multi-billion dollar company with an inscrutable design that may have earned its success *because* of its controversial UI. In her article,

[4]Kurt Wagner and Rani Molla, "Why Snapchat is shrinking," www.vox.com/2018/8/7/17661756/snap-earnings-snapchat-q2-instagram-user-growth.

"Did Snapchat succeed because of its controversial UI?" (`www.figma.com/blog/did-snapchat-succeed-because-of-its-controversial-ui/`), Carmel DeAmicis declared Snapchat a "design pioneer":

> *Despite the interface's insanity, some Snapchat features were major breakthroughs in design. It was the first big social app to open directly to the camera. That unconventional choice encouraged people to actually create their own content, instead of just consume others' posts.*

She also quotes Airbnb designer Ben Wilkins saying "The reason people love this is because it requires some level of tribal knowledge." It gives millennials "their own walled garden that their parents can't reach."

For the target audience in question, impenetrable design choices and rejecting standard patterns had an unusually positive effect on their product.

One particular and relevant quote I enjoyed was this:

> *"Some designers resent its success because it doesn't follow patterns we were taught to follow," said Tara Mann, a mobile designer at Basecamp, a project management tool.*

Sometimes it's OK to break the rules. The only way to know for sure though is to actually test the difference. By benchmarking your product's UI, you'll be able to find out if an innovation improves or detracts from the original experience.

How to break the rules

If you've decided that you want to try something more adventurous, first, you have to know the rules to break them. Before throwing out the rule book, consider the strengths of the patterns to date and understand them in all their detail.

Next, consider how ambitious your alternative approach is. When choosing between incremental and radical design improvements (`www.nngroup.com/articles/radical-incremental-redesign/`), breaking patterns are more radical changes, so you want to achieve a greater margin of improvement over a smaller, incremental change. Your radical innovation needs to achieve a 30% improvement in your measurable outcomes. Julio Zhuo, a product designer at Facebook, proposes a more conservative figure in her article, "Good Design" (`https://medium.com/the-year-of-the-looking-glass/good-design-a89c15136ba6`):

> *Obviousness comes from conforming to people's existing mental models. Don't waste time reinventing common UI patterns or paradigms unless they are at least 2x better, or you have some critical brand reason to do so.*

> —Julie Zhuo

She cites Microsoft OneNote product founder, Chris Pratley:

> *You know you have a good design when you show it to people and they say, "oh, yeah, of course," like the solution was obvious.*

> —Chris Pratley

In these examples you can see the appeal of conservative adherence to conventions and design patterns. Even then, one yardstick of a new approach's success might be if people still say, "oh, yeah, of course." Like the solution was obvious.

One sign that a successful radical innovation may be available is a change in technology. As voice-user interfaces become more reliable, we're likely to see greater shifts in interaction as new opportunities become available. Maybe this is the time to quash hamburger basements and instead *ask* the web page to access standard menu items, such as the "About page," or simply ask, "tell me about this company."

Before embarking on this adventure, you might evaluate how much slack you have in your system to shoulder the cost of any risky experiments. Can you afford to lose $1.3 billion of market share[5] if it goes wrong? If you cannot bear the impact, you might mitigate the risk by running smaller experiments or isolating smaller parts of the innovation to test. For example, you might independently validate UI copy out of context, test user flow using paper prototypes, and test usability in an interactive prototype before building a new alternative to a design pattern.

As I mentioned before, when you're about to implement radical innovations, user test the UI before and after. If you have no prior UI to benchmark because you're creating a new product, consider benchmarking a competitor's product. You can also track the impact of your radical design changes on your key measurable outcomes, such as sales and conversion rates. In this way you can prove that the alternative is better for key outcomes as well as qualitative perceived experience and satisfaction.

When to break patterns in design systems

In a design system, there's typically one execution of a pattern. A button, for example, is usually done one way, on purpose, to achieve consistent and predictable UI. How then does an individual UX designer engaged with a design system make the decision to break from the mold? In three cases:

- When consistency isn't achieving predictability, break the pattern.

- When consistency is detrimental, break the pattern.

- When behavior is different, elements should look different—this demands a different pattern.

---

[5]Dottie Schrock, "Snapchat: Our Take on the Design Kylie Called 'So Sad,'" www.leanplum.com/blog/app-engagement-snapchat/, March 2018.

Conversely, when should a designer stick to the system? When you see either of these two signs:

- When inconsistency is inconspicuous, causing users to ask "why" something looks different in one place to another, even though they behave the same (or too similarly)

- When the behavior is identical

For a rule of thumb, aim to be cohesive not consistent. Context trumps consistency when the design is still clearly in line with the spirit of the system, giving the impression of consistency and predictability, even with slight differences. Strong principles can help you here. If you have a design principle like "Insightful even over efficient," you might choose a data visualization that brings to light new information, even over the standard visualization in your product that is faster to navigate.

That wraps up the main reasons to ditch a pattern and how to move ahead when you do. These won't address every design system or solve every debate, but they can help guide decisions.

Summary

In this chapter we explored how to blend multiple patterns together into a seamless interaction experience by finding complementary patterns, minimizing duplication of shared elements across patterns when combining them, and finding large functional combinations of patterns with a bigger scope than the patterns we've seen in previous chapters. These larger functional "patterns" tend to appear less often in design systems and especially rarely in built component libraries as they often appear only once or twice in a single product.

We examined the unique impact specific applications of patterns might have, such as wish lists and how they relate to favorites. As we discussed in Chapter 5, the "Overall pattern" is a design smell, and you'll likely find more value from separately describing your wish list pattern and favorite pattern rather than treating favorites as a parent to the wish list pattern in the unlikely event you have both in your design system.

Beyond mixing and matching patterns, we saw how to validate breaks from convention with user testing. You can identify a successful departure from convention when your audience still reports that it "feels obvious," "easy," or "intuitive." You can identify the need for breaking from convention when an identified usability problem proves the pattern is failing you in its current form.

Altogether, this chapter has highlighted nine approaches to mix and match patterns and when to break away from them, including in design systems, all through the lens of modern e-commerce products and contemporary digital design.

CHAPTER 7

Conclusion

Thanks for coming along on the journey with me exploring the wild world of UI patterns and their place in design systems. I've thoroughly enjoyed writing, researching, and sharing everything in this book. My hope is that you'll come away a sharper digital professional, with a new understanding of UI patterns—recurring solutions to digital interface problems in a context.

You've learned how to

- Find a pattern you can apply to a given UI problem

- Deconstruct patterns to understand them in depth, including their constraints

- Build design systems using practical UI patterns

- Spot anti-patterns and dark patterns and question design smells

- Mix and match patterns and break from convention in the right way

This will help you

- Produce intuitive products through consistency and familiarity

- Save time instead of starting from scratch

© Diana MacDonald 2019
D. MacDonald, *Practical UI Patterns for Design Systems*,
https://doi.org/10.1007/978-1-4842-4938-3_7

- Communicate design decisions with evidence to support solutions

- Use smart defaults without extensive product design experience

- Improve your users' experiences

- Scale growing business with design

As a professional, you've

1. Gained an understanding of product design foundations through seeing design processes brought to light, especially as they apply to growing organizations with evolving design systems

2. Learned how to fast-track design work via practical examples of patterns for a variety of real-world purposes

3. Leveled up the breadth of your skills and understanding through the illumination of user experience design concepts, such as usability, accessibility, microcopy, motion design, and information architecture

Looking to the future

I wanted to write this book to guide motivated, growing web designers. I also wanted to help improve the state of the industry, letting the web community spend more time at the cutting edge instead of reinventing the wheel of proven solutions. If this book has helped you, it would mean the world to me if you reached out to let me know.

When you're considering what's next, I suggest you signup to these:

- Design on Medium (`https://medium.com/topic/design`)

- Design Systems on Slack (`http://design.systems/slack/`)

- Design Systems News (`http://news.design.systems/`)

As a community, we can help each other by sharing what we've learned along the way. If you and your organization have established a new UI pattern, I invite you to write or speak about it. Share what you've learned and how you've proven a solution's effectiveness in your design's context. Together, we'll build a better experience for everyone.

APPENDIX

Suggested reading

Chapter 2

To learn more about the patterns and ideas in Chapter 2, here are some additional resources.

Newsletter signup:

- Think Your Site Needs CAPTCHA? Try These User-Friendly Alternatives (www.usertesting.com/blog/think-your-site-needs-captcha-try-these-user-friendly-alternatives/)

- Design the Email Newsletter SignUp Box That Works (http://rafaltomal.com/email-newsletter-signup-box-that-works/)

Validation feedback:

- Apple human interface guidelines for data entry (https://developer.apple.com/design/human-interface-guidelines/macos/user-interaction/data-entry/)

- Microsoft errors (https://docs.microsoft.com/en-gb/windows/desktop/uxguide/mess-error)

© Diana MacDonald 2019
D. MacDonald, *Practical UI Patterns for Design Systems*,
https://doi.org/10.1007/978-1-4842-4938-3

- Material Design text field errors (`https://material.io/design/components/text-fields.html#anatomy`)

- Strunk and White's, *The Elements of Style* (`www.gutenberg.org/ebooks/37134`)

Competitive analysis:

- Largest Internet companies (`https://en.wikipedia.org/wiki/List_of_largest_Internet_companies`)

- Largest tech companies (`https://en.wikipedia.org/wiki/List_of_the_largest_information_technology_companies`)

- Fortune 500 companies by revenue (`http://fortune.com/rankings/`)

- Alexa top 500 sites on the Web by traffic (`www.alexa.com/topsites`)

Notifications:

- Google's Android permissions (`https://material.io/design/platform-guidance/android-permissions.html`)

- Apple's Requesting Permission (`https://developer.apple.com/design/human-interface-guidelines/ios/app-architecture/requesting-permission/`)

Progressive reduction:

- The Characteristics of Minimalism in Web Design (`www.nngroup.com/articles/characteristics-minimalism/`)

For each of the types of resources introduced in Chapter 2, here are some specific resources.

Pattern collections:

- UI Patterns (http://ui-patterns.com/patterns/)

- UIPatterns.io (http://uipatterns.io/)

- Welie Patterns in Interaction Design (www.welie.com/patterns/index.php)

Pattern galleries:

- pttrns (https://pttrns.com/)

- Nicely Done (http://nicelydone.club/patterns/)

- InspirationUI > All Patterns (http://inspirationui.com/)

- Pattern Tap > Type (http://patterntap.com/patterntap)

- UXArchive > Tasks (http://uxarchive.com/)

- Interfaces Pro (https://interfaces.pro/product-page/)

Domain-specific galleries:

- Mobile:

  - Mobile Patterns (www.mobile-patterns.com/)

  - 11 User Input Patterns for Mobile (https://designmodo.com/user-input-patterns-mobile/)

- Email:

  - Really Good Emails (http://reallygoodemails.com/)

- E-commerce:

  - Baymard Institute (https://baymard.com/)

- Onboarding:

  - User onboarding (`www.useronboard.com/how-slack-onboards-new-users/`)

  - Empty states (`http://emptystat.es/`)

  - UXArchive (`http://uxarchive.com/tasks/onboarding`)

  - First-time UX (`http://firsttimeux.tumblr.com/`)

- Interaction design:

  - LittleBigDetails (`http://littlebigdetails.com/`)

  - Codrops blueprints (`https://tympanus.net/codrops/category/blueprints/`)

  - Codepen Collections (`https://codepen.io/topics/ui-pattern`)

- Social:

  - Yahoo Design Pattern Library > Social via the Wayback Machine (`https://web.archive.org/web/20160728011421/https:/developer.yahoo.com/ypatterns/`)

  - Designing Social Interfaces (`www.designingsocialinterfaces.com/patterns.wiki/index.php?title=Main_Page`)

  - UI-Patterns > Social (`http://ui-patterns.com/patterns/social/list`)

- Search:

  - Peter Morville's Flickr Search Patterns
    (www.flickr.com/photos/morville/
    collections/72157603785835882/) for
    Search Patterns (http://shop.oreilly.com/
    product/9780596802288.do)

Platform guidelines:

- Human Interface Guidelines (https://en.wikipedia.
  org/wiki/Human_interface_guidelines), such as

  - Apple's iOS guidelines (https://developer.apple.
    com/design/human-interface-guidelines/)

  - Elementary's guidelines (https://elementary.
    io/docs/human-interface-guidelines#human-
    interface-guidelines)

- Google's Material Design guidelines (https://
  material.io/design/)

- Microsoft's windows guidelines (https://docs.
  microsoft.com/en-gb/windows/desktop/uxguide/
  guidelines)

UI frameworks:

- Bootstrap (http://getbootstrap.com/components/)

- Zurb Foundation (http://foundation.zurb.com/
  sites/docs/kitchen-sink.html)

- Tachyons (http://tachyons.io/components/)

- Semantic UI (https://semantic-ui.com/
  introduction/glossary.html)

- Spectre (`https://picturepan2.github.io/spectre/components.html`)

- Element (`http://element.eleme.io/`)

- Skeleton (`http://getskeleton.com/`)

- Bit (`https://bit.dev/components`)

Inspiring visual style:

- Site Inspire (`www.siteinspire.com/`)

- Httpster (`http://httpster.net/`)

- Dribbble (`https://dribbble.com/`)

- Awwwards (`www.awwwards.com/`)

- IXDA (`http://awards.ixda.org/entries/`)

- Front-end awards (`https://thefwa.com/`)

- Page Flows (`https://pageflows.com/flow/onboarding`)

- One Page Love (`https://onepagelove.com/`)

- Land-book (`https://land-book.com/`)

- Collect UI (`http://collectui.com/`)

- Design Snips (`http://designsnips.com/category/inspiration/`)

Chapter 3

To learn more about SEO and UI, see Moz's Beginner's Guide to SEO (`https://moz.com/beginners-guide-to-seo`).

For a straightforward, practical guide to improving interface microcopy, see Effective Writing For Your UI: Things to Avoid by Nick

Babich (https://uxplanet.org/effective-writing-for-your-ui-things-to-avoid-f6084e94e009).

To learn about implementing design patterns accessibly, check out The A11Y Project (http://a11yproject.com/). For an in-depth reference, I refer you to Heydon Pickering's book, *Inclusive Design Patterns*.

Chapter 4

For your inspiration, here are some pattern library and design system resources, loosely grouped into the types of guides they are.

Editorial style guides:

- The Guardian and Observer Style Guide (www.theguardian.com/info/series/guardian-and-observer-style-guide)

- MailChimp Content Style Guide (http://styleguide.mailchimp.com/)

- Intuit QuickBooks: Voice and tone guide (https://designsystem.quickbooks.com/voice-and-tone/)

Brand guides:

- Website Style Guide Resources (http://styleguides.io/)

- Style guides (https://designschool.canva.com/blog/50-meticulous-style-guides-every-startup-see-launching/)

- Brand style guides (https://saijogeorge.com/brand-style-guide-examples/)

- Lonely Planet style guide (https://rizzo.lonelyplanet.com/styleguide/design-elements/colours)

- Ubuntu's brand guidelines (https://design.ubuntu.com/brand)

Design guidelines and visual language:

- Find Guidelines (`http://findguidelin.es/`)

- Apple's design principles (`https://developer.apple.com/ios/human-interface-guidelines/overview/design-principles/`)

- IBM's Design Language (`www.ibm.com/design/language/`)

- Wikimedia design style guide (`https://design.wikimedia.org/style-guide/index.html`)

Pattern libraries or front-end style guides:

- Hillary Clinton's internal Pantsuit pattern library (`https://medium.com/git-out-the-vote/pantsuit-the-hillary-clinton-ui-pattern-library-238e9bf06b54`), which is not publicly accessible

- MailChimp's pattern library (`https://ux.mailchimp.com/patterns`)

- Walmart's web style guide (`http://walmartlabs.github.io/web-style-guide/`)

- Yelp (`www.yelp.com/styleguide`)

- Buzzfeed's CSS style guide like BassCSS (`http://solid.buzzfeed.com/`)

- Code for America (`https://style.codeforamerica.org/`)

Living style guides:

- Living Style Guide generator gem
  (`https://livingstyleguide.org/`)

- KSS (Knyle Style Sheets) (`https://warpspire.com/kss/`)

- Living style guide and pattern library generators
  (`https://github.com/davidhund/styleguide-generators`)

Code style guides:

- Mozilla Developer Network: Coding style (`https://developer.mozilla.org/en-US/docs/Mozilla/Developer_guide/Coding_Style`)

- Code Guide by @mdo (Mark Otto) for HTML and CSS
  (`http://codeguide.co/`)

- CSS Guidelines by Harry Roberts (`https://cssguidelin.es/`)

- Google's Style Guides (`https://github.com/google/styleguide`)

Component libraries:

- Awesome React components (`https://github.com/brillout/awesome-react-components`)

- Pure UI (`https://rauchg.com/2015/pure-ui`)

- U.S. Web Design System (`https://designsystem.digital.gov/components/`)

- Pivotal UI (`http://styleguide.cfapps.io/index.html`)

- Shopify's Polaris components (`https://polaris.shopify.com/components/get-started`)

Design systems:

- Salesforce's Lightning Design System (`www.lightningdesignsystem.com/guidelines/overview/`)

- Google's Material Design (`https://material.io/guidelines/material-design/introduction.html`)

- Shopify's Polaris design system (`https://polaris.shopify.com/`)

- Atlassian's design system (`https://atlassian.design/`)

- GE's Predix design system (`www.predix-ui.com/#/home`)

- FutureLearn's design system (`www.futurelearn.com/pattern-library`)

- Intuit's QuickBooks design system (`https://designsystem.quickbooks.com/`)

- BBC's Global Experience Language (`www.bbc.co.uk/gel`)

- GOV.UK service manual (`www.gov.uk/service-manual`)

Other design system resources:

- Adele, UXPin's "repository of publicly available design systems and pattern libraries" (`https://adele.uxpin.com/`)

- Design Systems Repo (`https://designsystemsrepo.com/design-systems/`)

- Awesome Design Systems on GitHub (`https://github.com/alexpate/awesome-design-systems/blob/master/README.md`)

- Design Systems Handbook: Building Design Systems (`www.designbetter.co/design-systems-handbook/building-design-system`)

- Clarity Conference (`www.clarityconf.com/`)

- Government design systems (`http://government.github.io/best-practices/design-systems/`)

- Airbnb's design system (`http://airbnb.design/the-way-we-build/`)

- Design systems are for people by Jina Anne (`https://publication.design.systems/design-systems-are-for-people-a484620b6988`)

Chapter 5

Hamburger menus or hamburger basements make for a fascinating case study of anti-patterns. Here are some suggested readings to learn more.

- When To Use a Hamburger Menu (`http://babich.biz/hamburger-good-ux/`)

- Top 3 IA Questions about Navigation Menus (`www.nngroup.com/articles/ia-questions-navigation-menus/`)

- The Thumb Zone: Designing For Mobile Users (`www.smashingmagazine.com/2016/09/the-thumb-zone-designing-for-mobile-users/`)

- Why Content Reigns Supreme In UX Design (`www.fastcodesign.com/3054090/why-content-reigns-supreme-in-ux-design`)

- Long-Term Exposure to Flat Design: How the Trend Slowly Decreases User Efficiency (`www.nngroup.com/articles/flat-design-long-exposure/`)

- The Ultimate Guide to the Hamburger Menu and Its Alternatives (`https://uxplanet.org/the-ultimate-guide-to-the-hamburger-menu-and-its-alternatives-e2da8dc7f1db`)

- Are Users Ready for the Desktop Hamburger Icon? (`www.sitepoint.com/are-users-ready-for-the-desktop-hamburger-icon/`)

- Why Users Click Content Links More Than Menus (`https://uxmovement.com/navigation/why-users-click-content-links-more-than-menus/`)

Index

A

Printed in the United States
By Bookmasters